公元787年，唐封疆大吏马总集诸子精华，编著成《意林》一书6卷，流传至今

意林：始于公元787年，距今1200余年

U0871489

意林®

一则故事　改变一生

米德兰中学
Midland School

米德兰中学（Midland School）拥有80多年历史，其中33%左右的老师具备高级教师资格证，研究生以上学历。该校教育严格，作风要求高，多年来坚持小班教学的风格。

米德兰中学占地将近120公顷，拥有3座教学楼，2座实验楼，1座图书馆，3座宿舍楼，2座体育场馆，1座健身房。米德兰中学紧挨着全美综合排名第44位的加州大学圣巴巴拉分校，学生可以选择去该所大学图书馆内借书，并且选择指定的先修课程。

学校以民风淳朴而著称，学校坐落于大草原，学校的建筑以原木搭建，坚持低碳环保的原则。学生在学校内，需要自己洗衣服，清理食堂。学生在学校有一些额外的课程，如骑马，建筑学等。

米尔布鲁克学校
Millbrook School

米尔布鲁克学校（Millbrook School）创立于1931年，位于纽约市以北145千米，是一所男女合校的私立走读寄宿制中学。学校的办学理念是通过培养学生在德、智、体、知、情、意等方面的协调发展从而塑造一个不仅自足而且对社会有用的人。

米尔布鲁克学校是一家小型的大学预科男女寄宿学校，现有学生250人。严格的传统课程包括荣誉课程、升学课程、选修课程以及其他独立的学习机会，如艺术和科学的野外考查、知名人士论坛等。所有学生都要参加为期一周的短期旅行以培养校外的学习兴趣。

米尔布鲁克学校拥有324公顷，有湿地、木板路、自然林、2.4公顷的特雷弗国家动物园、天文台和气象站。这些资源为学生学习科学提供了很大的便利。特雷弗动物园已经成为对科学感兴趣的学生的活实验室，在那里，濒危物种受到了保护和照顾、受伤或生病的野生动物也得到了医治。

圣安妮贝尔菲尔德中学
St. Anne’s–Belfield School

圣安妮贝尔菲尔德中学（St. Anne’s-Belfield School）成立于1910年，是一所有着优良传统的住宿男女合校，学校很重视荣誉、个人特质及优点。学校设有15门先修课程，也有著名大学预备课程暑期课程。学校着重艺术，培养学生的价值观、学习技能、自信心及领导能力。

圣安妮贝尔菲尔德中学有以下设施：6栋教学楼、3个图书馆(藏书大约23,000册)、3个体育馆、2个人造操场、3片草地、1个棒球场、1个垒球场、6个网球场及5个壁球场。

绝大部分国际生都选择七天住校的方式，这样，他们可以拥有一个很好的语言和文化环境。老师和舍监可以帮助每位学生并引导他们适应新环境，但还是需要学生自己主动去参加各种社交活动。

雅典娜中学
The Athenian School

雅典娜中学（The Athenian School）为男女同校的全日制寄宿中学。小班授课制（平均每班有15名学生），着重于每个学生的个性培养。课程设计人性化，并为学生提供多次社会实践的机会，让学生走出校园，更早的适应社会，树立起他们可以在世界舞台上驰骋的信心。

坐落于加州山脚下，占地75公顷的雅典娜中学是离旧金山海湾区最近的仅有的一所无任何宗教派别的寄宿学校。每年招收的学生中，国际学生占10%，为英语是非母语的学生营造了很好的语言环境。同时为国际学生设立母语非英语语言课程，以更快的提高他们的英语能力，为将来进入大学做好准备。

毕业生去向：哥伦比亚大学，哈佛大学，普林斯顿大学，斯坦福大学等美国著名高校。

全世界最美的课文

世界语文·美国语文

International Literature American Literature

2

《意林》编辑部　主编

轩辕心云　时小鱼　译

吉林摄影出版社

·长春·

全世界最美的课文系列

图书在版编目（CIP）数据

世界语文. 美国语文. 2 / 《意林》编辑部主编 ；轩辕心云，时小鱼译. -- 长春 ： 吉林摄影出版社，2014.3

ISBN 978-7-5498-1974-4

Ⅰ. ①世… Ⅱ. ①意… ②轩… ③时… Ⅲ. ①故事－作品集－美国 Ⅳ. ①I11

中国版本图书馆CIP数据核字(2014)第039511号

世界语文·美国语文2 SHIJIE YUWEN MEIGUO YUWEN 2

主　　编　《意林》编辑部
译　　者　轩辕心云　时小鱼
出 版 人　孙洪军
总 策 划　杜　务
主　　编　孙洪军　顾　平
责任编辑　施　岚　胡晓路
丛书统筹　蔡　燕
策划编辑　邓志娟
执行编辑　邓志娟
封面设计　李　倩
美术编辑　孔凡雷
开　　本　700mm×1000mm 1/16
字　　数　280千字
印　　张　16.25
印　　数　1～20000册
版　　次　2014年3月第1版
印　　次　2014年3月第1次印刷

出　　版　吉林摄影出版社
发　　行　吉林摄影出版社
地　　址　长春市泰来街1825号
邮　　编　130062
电　　话　总编办：0431-86012616
发 行 科　0431-86012602
网　　址　www.jlsycbs.cn
经　　销　全国各地新华书店
印　　刷　北京天宇万达印刷有限公司

书　　号　ISBN 978-7-5498-1974-4　　　　定　　价：25.90 元

启　事

本书编选时参阅了部分报刊和著作，我们未能与部分作品的文字作者、漫画作者以及插画作者取得联系，在此深表歉意。请各位作者见到本书后及时与我们联系，以便按国家相关规定支付稿酬及赠送样书。

地址：北京市朝阳区南磨房路37号华腾北搪商务大厦1501室《意林》编辑部（100022）

电话：010-51908602

CONTENTS 目录

第一章 NO.1 美国故事 American Stories

第二章 NO.2
精英人物
The Elites

第四章
NO.4

动物长征
Marching Animals

第五章
NO.5

科海迷途
Mysterious Science

第六章 NO.6 繁星集
A Myriad of Stars

英汉对照

世界语文·美国语文

International Literature American Literature

2

【第一章】

NO.1

美国故事

American Stories

世界语文·美国语文

International Literature American Literature

2

一块蕾丝桌布的奇迹
The Gold and Ivory Tablecloth

圣诞节期间，美国全国各地的男人和女人都会聚集到教堂，去了解发生在这个世界上的最伟大的奇迹。今天我要讲的这个故事却不能称之为一个奇迹——至少不完全是。

故事的男主人公是一位年轻的牧师。他所在的教堂已经破败不堪。在很久之前，这座教堂也曾有过富丽堂皇的岁月，之前它被建造得宏伟壮丽。一些名人曾在那里的讲道坛上激情布道，也曾在圣坛前虔心祈祷。不管富人还是穷人，都曾在那里做过礼拜。如今，教堂所在的小镇已经不见昔日的繁华，但是牧师和他年轻的妻子对这座破落的教堂还充满着希望。他们认为，通过油漆、榔头，还有坚定的信念，他们一定能够让教堂恢复往日的风采。就这样，他们着手对教堂的修整工作。

然而，天有不测风云，在十二月下半旬的时候，一场突如其来的暴风雨席卷了整个河谷，给这座小小的教堂带来了最严重的破坏——因为大雨的侵袭，圣坛正后面的石灰墙吸足了雨水，剥落了一大块。牧师和他的妻子心情沮丧地清扫了暴风雨肆虐后的一地狼藉，但是对于那个因墙面剥落造成的难看的大洞，他们却无计可施。他的妻子流下了眼泪，“还有两天就是圣诞节了！”牧师看了看那个洞，感到沮丧，很快地他提醒自己，“这可能是上帝的旨意！”

现在，那场暴风雨带来的积极的一面已经显现出来。

那天下午，心情沮丧的夫妻二人参加了一个为某个青年组织举行的拍卖会。拍卖商打开一个盒子，从中抖出一块很漂亮的黄白色的蕾丝桌布。这块桌布看起来相当华丽，几乎有4.5米长。但是，因为年深日久，桌布看起来有些陈旧过时。如今它还能派上什么用场呢？只有为数不多的人开始喊价了，但是表现得并不热心。牧师突然想到一个很好的主意。他用6美元50美分将桌布拍了下来。

他将桌布带回教堂，用大头钉将它挂在了圣坛后面的墙上，正好将那个大洞完全遮住。

这真是一个绝妙的搭配。他满怀喜悦地继续准备他的圣诞节布道。

就在平安夜的那个中午，当牧师打开教堂大门的时候，他注意到一个女人正冒着严寒站在公共汽车站。

“公共汽车至少40分钟以后才到这里！”他喊道，然后邀请她到教堂里来取暖。

她告诉他说她因为要来这个镇上一户有钱人家应聘做家庭教师，所以一大早就从市里赶过来了，但是最终遭到了拒绝。她是因为战争流亡到美国的，英语讲得有点儿蹩脚。

那个女人在一条长凳上坐下来，一边休息，一边搓着双手取暖。过了一会儿，她低下头，开始祈祷。当牧师开始调整那块蕾丝桌布在墙上的位置的时候，她抬起头。突然之间，她站起来，走过圣坛前的台阶，然后紧盯着桌布。牧师微微一笑，向她讲述了那场暴风雨带来的破坏。但是她似乎没有在听牧师的话。她拿起桌布的一个褶皱处，用手指将它展平。

“这是我的！”她说。“这是我的宴会桌布！”她举起桌布一角，向一脸惊诧的牧师展示绣在那上面的姓名的首字母。“这块桌布是我丈夫专门在布鲁塞尔为我定制的！世界上不可能有同样的第二块！”

在接下来的时间里，那个女人和牧师兴奋地交谈起来。她说她是维也纳人，她和丈夫因为反对纳粹的统治，所以被迫离开了自己的祖国。为了安全起见，有人建议他们分头行动。她丈夫送她上了一列开往瑞士的火车。他们计划一旦他把行李装上轮船送出来，就尽快和她会合。没想到那一别竟成了永别。后来，她听说他死在了一个纳粹集中营里。

“我一直认为那是我的过错——我不应该一个人离开，”她说，“这些年的颠沛流离可能就是对我的惩罚吧。”

牧师试图去安慰她，并劝她把桌布带走。她拒绝了他的建议，然后离开了。

平安夜的晚上，教堂里挤满了人。很明显，那块桌布发挥了极其重要的作用。通过牧师精心的安排，它在烛光下看起来真是棒极了。

布道以后，牧师站在走廊上。很多人告诉他说教堂看起来漂亮极了。一个绅士模样的中年男人——他是当地一位钟表修理工——却是一脸困惑的样子。

“太奇怪了，”他用柔和的声音说。“很多年前，我的妻子——愿上帝使她安息——和我有一块同样的桌布。在我们在维也纳的家里，我妻子把它铺在餐桌上，”说到这里，他脸上露出微笑，“不过只有主教来吃晚餐的时候才会如此！”听到这些，牧师突然激动起来。他向钟表匠讲述了那天早些时候来教堂取暖的那个女人的故事。

惊愕的钟表匠一把抓住牧师的胳膊。“这是真的吗？她真的还活着？”

两个男人一起找到了曾经面试她的那个家庭。然后，他们坐上牧师的汽车，一起来到那座城市。当圣诞节来临的时候，这个男人和他的妻子在经历那么多悲伤的圣诞节后，终于重逢了。

任何听了这个故事的人都觉得那个被暴风雨侵蚀出来的大洞带来的是令人欢喜的结果。当然，人们会说这是个奇迹，但是我认为你应该会同意这句话：这本就是一个收获奇迹的季节！

The Gold and Ivory Tablecloth

At Christmastime, men and women everywhere gather in their churches to wonder a new at the greatest miracle the world has ever known. But the story I like best to recall was not a miracle—not exactly.

It happened to a pastor who was very young. His church was very old. Once, long ago, it had flourished. Famous men had preached from its pulpit, prayed before its altar. Rich and poor alike had worshiped there and built it beautifully. Now the good days had passed from the section of town where it stood. But the pastor and his young wife believed in their run-down church. They felt that with paint, hammer, and faith, they could get it in shape. Together they went to work.

But late in December, a severe storm whipped through the river valley, and the worst blow fell on the little church—a huge chunk of rain—soaked plaster fell out of the inside wall just behind the altar. Sorrowfully the pastor and his wife swept away the mess, but they couldn't hide the ragged hole. The pastor looked at it and had to remind himself quickly, "Thy will be done!"

The joyful purpose of the storm that had knocked a hole in the wall of the church was now quite clear.

But his wife wept, “Christmas is only two days away!”

That afternoon the dispirited couple attended an auction held for the benefit of a youth group. The auctioneer opened a box and shook out of its folds a handsome gold-and-ivory lace tablecloth. It was a magnificent item, nearly 15 feet long. But it, too, dated from a long-vanished era. Who, today, had any use for such a thing? There were a few halfhearted bids. Then the pastor was seized with what he thought was a great idea. He bid it in for six dollars and fifty cents.

He carried the cloth back to the church and tacked it up on the wall behind the altar. It completely hid the hole! It was a great triumph. Happily he went back to preparing his Christmas sermon.

Just before noon on the day of Christmas Eve, as the pastor was opening the church, he noticed a woman standing in the cold at the bus stop.

“The bus won’t be here for 40 minutes!” he called, and he invited her into the church to get warm.

She told him that she had come from the city that morning to be interviewed for a job as governess to the children of one of the wealthy families in town but she had been turned down. A war refugee, she had imperfect English.

The woman sat down in a pew and chafed her hands and rested. After a while, she dropped her head and prayed. She looked up as the pastor began to adjust the great gold-and-ivory lace cloth across the hole. She rose suddenly and walked up the steps of the chancel. She looked at the tablecloth. The pastor smiled and started to tell her about the storm damage, but she didn't seem to listen. She took up a fold of the cloth and rubbed it between her fingers.

"It is mine!" she said. "It is my banquet cloth!" She lifted up a corner and showed the surprised pastor that there were initials monogrammed on it. "My husband had the cloth made especially for me in Brussels! There could not be another like it!"

For the next few minutes, the woman and the pastor talked excitedly together. She explained that she was Viennese, that she and her husband had opposed the Nazis and decided to leave the country. They were advised to go separately. Her husband put her on a train for Switzerland. They planned that he would join her as soon as he could arrange to ship their household goods across the border.

She never saw him again. Later she heard that he had died in a concentration camp.

"I have always felt that it was my fault—to leave without him," she said. "Perhaps these years of wandering have been my punishment!"

The pastor tried to comfort her, urged her to take the cloth with her. She refused. Then she went away.

As the church began to fill on Christmas Eve, it was clear that the cloth was going to be a great success. It had been skillfully designed to look its best by candlelight.

After the service, the pastor stood at the doorway; many people told him that the church looked beautiful. One gentle-faced, middle-aged man—he was the local clock-and-watch repairman—looked rather puzzled.

"It is strange," he said in his soft accent. "Many years ago, my wife—God rest her—and I owned such a cloth. In our home in Vienna, my wife put it on the table"—and here he smiled—"only when the bishop came to dinner!"

The pastor suddenly became very excited. He told the jeweler about the woman who had been in church earlier in the day.

The startled jeweler clutched the pastor's arm. "Can it be? Does she live?"

Together the two got in touch with the family who had interviewed her. Then, in the pastor's car, they started for the city. And as Christmas Day was born, this man and his wife—who had been separated through so many saddened Yuletides—were reunited.

To all who heard this story, the joyful purpose of the storm that had knocked a hole in the wall of the church was now quite clear. Of course, people said it was a miracle, but I think you will agree it was the season for it!

"The Gold & Ivory Tablecloth" is one of 38 uplifting tales in the Reader's Digest Treasury of Joy and Inspiration. This collector's item features editors' selections of our most powerful true stories, miracles, and dramas in real life, including works by Christopher Reeve, James Michener, and Billy Crystal. To learn more or buy a copy, go toreadersdigest.com/joy.

美国历史
American History

我们九年级全体同学都来到了公立十三中学封闭的操场上。学校给了我们“自由”活动时间；我们的体育老师德帕尔马先生要求我们一直保持“活动状态”。这就意味着女孩们要一直跳绳，男孩们要在操场尽头的篮球架那里一直练投篮。与此同时，他会在教学楼内密切地“监视我们的一举一动”。

记得那天非常阴冷，预示着帕特森将要迎来它的第一场雪。我感到非常难受，因为我忘了带手套出来。在玩跳绳的过程中，我的指关节变得通红，并且疼得厉害。此外，我还遭到那些黑人女孩的谩骂，因为她们怪我没有卖力地摇绳子以配合她们跳绳的节奏。

“嘿，瘦猴子，用点儿劲儿。你今天一点儿力气也没有吗？”那个叫盖尔的最高大的黑人女孩负责跳绳的另一端，她冲我吼道，“今天的早餐你没有吃米饭、豆子和猪排吗？”

其他的女孩一哄而笑，用猪排这个词唱起了顺口溜：“猪排，猪排，你有没有吃猪排？”跳双绳的时候，她们成双结对地入绳，轻捷地出绳，既不会被绳子打到，也不会乱了节奏。我感到两颊发烫，接着我的眼镜蒙上了雾气，我的视线开始变得模糊。我没有办法和盖尔协调一致地摇动绳子了。寒冷像往常一样侵入我的骨髓，让我忍不住哭了起来。我感到丢脸极了。我恨这座城市，尤其是它的冬天。我恨我所在的公立十三中学。我恨自己瘦骨嶙峋，胸部平平；我嫉妒那些黑人女孩，她们跳绳的速度真快，看得人眼花缭乱。在我被冻得瑟瑟发抖的时候，她们总是看起来暖暖和和的。

九年级那年，我生活中唯一一个美好和光明的来源就是能够见到尤金，这也是我对新学期唯一的期待。八月份的时候，尤金和他的家人搬进了我所在街区唯一一座有院子和树的房子里。从我所住的E1公寓的卧室窗户就可以看到他的家。事实上，如果我坐在消防梯上，那么尤金家的后院就在我正下方。夏天的时候，我最喜欢坐在那里读我从图书馆借来的书。那个八月以前，一对犹太老夫妻一直住在这座房子里。在过去的几年里，我已经在他们不知道的情况下变成了他们家庭的一员。我能看到他们的厨房和后院；虽然我听不到他们的对话，但是我知道他们什么时候在争吵，也知道他们其中一个什么时候生病了，还有诸如此类的其他很多事情。这些情况都是我在他们吃饭的时候通过观察他们得到的。我能够看到他们的餐桌、水槽和炉灶。在他们和平相处的时候，老先生会坐在桌边读报纸，而老妇人则在一旁准备饭菜。如果他们吵架的话，老先生会离开厨房，留下老妇人一个人双眼发呆地在那里坐很长时间。如果他们其中一个生病了，另外一个就会到厨房来拿东西，然后用托盘端出去。老先生在六月份去世了。上学期的最后一周我没有看到他坐在餐桌旁，然后有一天我看到厨房里挤满了人。最后，老妇人在一个身材敦实的中年女人的搀扶下走出了那座房子。以前，我曾经看到过那个中年女人几次，可能是老妇人的女儿吧。然后一个男人拿出来几个行李箱。之后那座房子就空置了好几周。我真想爬到他们的院子里，去给那些曾被老妇人精心照料过的花儿们浇浇水。

尤金一家搬进来的时候，那个院子已经荒草丛生。尤金的父亲花了好几天的时间在院子里割草。待他把杂草清除完之后，从我坐的地方已经看不到那些红色、黄色和紫色的花簇了。我从来没有看到过这家人一起坐在厨房的餐桌旁用餐。厨房里只有尤金那个红头发的高个子妈妈身穿一身白色制服在忙活，我猜她穿的是护士服。而他的爸爸总是在我还没有起床的时候就早早出家门了，我从来没有看到过他在餐厅用餐。只有在周末的时候，我偶尔才能看到他：在大橡树下的草坪上有一张躺椅，他们会坐在躺椅上。每个人都把脸埋在一份报纸后面，尤金也在那里。尤金个子很高，长着一头金发，还戴着眼镜。我很快就对尤金产生了好感，因为他会坐在餐桌边，连续读几个小时的书。那个夏天，虽然我们从来没有跟彼此说过一句话，但是我一直在消防梯上跟他做伴。

开学以后，我跑遍了我所有课程所在的教室，希望能够找到尤金。但是公立十三中校园很大，学生很多，我用了几天时间，小心翼翼地问了许多人之后才发现尤金所学的科目都是荣誉课程。虽然我是个全A生，却没有资格注册荣誉课程，因为英语不是我的母语。经过一番精心策划，我和他有过几次“偶遇”：在他的衣物柜所在的走廊；在我上课的教学楼的对面，在图书馆自修室，等等。数次“偶遇”后，他终于在图书馆的自修教室第一次注意到我，但是并没有开口说话。最后，某天放学回家的路上，虽然我紧张得胃抽筋，还是决定直接向他走过去。

我已经做好了会被他势利地拒绝的准备。当我走向他时，我因为紧张不安有些气喘吁吁。我脱口而出：“你是尤金，对吧？”他向我微微一笑，向上推了推鼻梁上的眼镜，然后点点头。我看到他的脸“唰”地红了。尤金也喜欢我，但是他太害羞了。那天，大部分时间都是我在讲话。他不断地点头和微笑。在接下来的几周时间里，我们放学后都是一起回家。他会在E1公寓的拐角徘徊一会儿，然后走向自己那幢两层楼的家。直到尤金一家搬进去之后我才发现E1公寓挡住了他们家的大部分阳光，唯一得光的地方就是那位老妇人曾经种花的那片小小的土地。

我没有告诉尤金我能从卧室看到他家厨房这件事。我觉得自己很不诚实，但是我喜欢偷偷地看着他，与他分享宁静的夜晚，尤其是我们在学校的图书馆一起借书时我了解了他所读的书后，我更想保守这个秘密。

一天，当我坐在卧室的窗台上凝视窗外的时候，我母亲走了进来，用她一贯粗鲁的方式说道："埃莱娜，你在发什么愣呀？"其实她想说的是入神，就是女孩那种愚蠢的迷恋。自从我十四岁开始来月经后，母亲就开始对我的事特别警惕，好像如果不整天看着我并且对我唠叨行为举止要像位淑女，我就会做出一些疯狂或者出格的事情。她不断地向我灌输贞操、道德之类的思想，但是我对这些话题一点儿兴趣也没有。我知道母亲在帕特森过得很不开心，但是父亲在帕塞伊克的牛仔裤厂有一份很好的差事，他一直向我们保证，我们全家很快就能够搬到那里，住进一座属于我们自己的房子里。周日的时候，我们全家就会开车到帕特森、克利夫顿和帕塞伊克的郊外。夏天的时候去有人刈草的地方，冬天的时候去有孩子堆雪人的地方，那些地方的雪是洁白无瑕的，而帕特森市区到处都是灰色的雪泥，似乎从天空中飘落下来的时候就是那个颜色。我已经学会倾听父母用西班牙语谈论他们如童话般的梦想，比如在我出生前，他们生活在天堂岛屿波多黎各生活的故事。当我还是个小女孩的时候，我曾经去过波多黎各。当时是去参加我祖母的葬礼，记忆里只有那些号啕大哭的一身黑衣的女人。我母亲哭得太过伤心，在被喂食一粒药丸后，她昏睡了足足两天时间。而我被一群自称我的阿姨、叔叔、堂兄弟姐妹的陌生人围着，感觉像迷路了一样，不知如何是好。所以，我还是很高兴能够再次返回帕特森市。从那以后，我们就再也没有回去过，虽然我的父母一直在讨论将来某天在那座岛屿的海滩边上买一座房子，在那里度过退休后的时光——这是住在E1公寓所有居民共同的梦想。对于我而言，我的梦想则是上大学，将来当一名教师。

但是在遇到尤金以后，我更多地考虑现在的快乐而不是将来的梦想。现在我最想做的事情就是走进那座我已经观察了好几年的房子，我想看看那对老夫妻曾经住过的其他房间，以及尤金的房间。最重要的是，我希望和尤金像两个成年人一样一起坐在餐桌旁，像那位老先生和老妇人一样，一起喝喝咖啡，讨论讨论书籍。我已经开始读《飘》。我完全被书中的内容吸引住了，尤其是书中那个勇敢热情的漂亮女孩，她住在一座大宅子里，有深爱她的父母和什么事情都帮她打理的奴隶。我不相信世界上曾有过这样的地方。我想问尤金一些问题，因为他曾经说过他和他父母就来自佐治亚州，而那部小说的故事就是发生在这个州。尤金全家因为他父亲工作的需要才搬到了帕特森，他的母亲对此很不开心。尤金用迷人的声音向我讲述这些事情。他说话一字一顿，给人一种奇特而又欢快的感觉。学校里的孩子都叫他“乡巴佬”，并取笑他说话的方式。我知道我是他唯一的朋友，虽然我为他感到难过，却暗自欣喜。每当我们两个人走在一起的时候，大家就会喊我们“瘦猴”和“乡巴佬”。

德帕尔马先生把我们召集到操场上的那个阴冷天就是肯尼迪总统遇刺的那天。德帕尔马先生身材矮小，肌肉发达，一头黑发向下梳得整整齐齐的。他是我们的科学老师、体育教练兼训导师。那些惹了麻烦的学生都会被分派到他负责的训导室，接受他的训话。他还负责平息操场上的打斗，以及押送那些愤怒的学生去办公室。另外，德帕尔马先生还负责“约见”学生的父母。

那天，他站在主要由黑人和波多黎各孩子组成的两列学生前面。时过十一月，帕特森的天气一天比一天寒冷，被要求“保持运动”的学生们因为长时间待在寒冷的户外开始变得暴躁不堪。让我们震惊不已的是，德帕尔马先生竟然当着我们的面哭泣起来。不是那种成年人的默默落泪，而是痛苦的啜泣。队列的后面发出了“哧哧”的笑声。我当时也站在后面，被冻得瑟瑟发抖。

“听着。”德帕尔马先生将双臂举过头顶，像要指挥一支乐队似的。他的声音有些颤抖，他用双手遮住了面部，他那宽阔的胸膛剧烈地起伏着。我后面的某个学生“咯咯”笑出了声。

“听着，”他重复道，“发生了一件可怕的事。”他的喉咙发出一种奇怪的咕噜声。他转过身去，向身后的水泥墙吐了一口唾沫。

“真恶心！”有人说道。大家听了之后都笑了。

“我们的总统死了，你们这些蠢货。我早就应该知道这个消息对一群像你们这样的失败者而言根本不会意味着什么。滚回家去吧。”他开始叫嚷起来。有那么一两分钟的时间，大家都站着一动不动。紧接着，一个大女孩大叫一声“好耶”，便冲出队列去拿靠放在教学楼砖墙边的课本。其他人紧随其后，争先恐后地拿自己的东西，乱作一团。当时离放学铃声响起还有一个小时。

我感到有些害怕，慢慢向E1公寓走去。街道上给人一种阴森恐怖的感觉。路过马里奥的杂货店的时候，我向里面看了看。那里向来是高中生们最爱集聚的地方，可是这次我只看到两个年迈的犹太男人。他们正在苏打吧台那里用有些生气的语调与快餐厨师交谈。他们说话的声音很低，我听不清楚他们在谈些什么，甚至帕特森交通最繁忙的路口的车辆都比往日行驶得缓慢，而且听不到任何汽车喇叭声。往日里，E1公寓的那群失业人员总是聚集在公寓楼前的台阶上，使得女人们进出楼都成问题。那天，E1公寓楼前的台阶前却看不到他们的身影。走廊上那些敞开的门里也没有传出嘈杂的音乐声。我走进家门之后，发现母亲正坐在模糊不清的电视机屏幕前。

她抬起满是泪痕的脸看了看我，说道："我的天哪！"然后又转向电视机屏幕，好像那里有东西在牵引着她的视线。我走进了自己的房间。

虽然我也想对肯尼迪总统的死表示悲伤难过，却没有办法抑制心中的喜悦和兴奋，因为今天我要去尤金家。他邀请我放学后到他家里和他一起为美国历史课的考试作准备。我们还打算一起走路去图书馆呢。我低头看了看他家的后院：橡树的叶子已经落光了，地面因为结冰而看起来灰溜溜的。他家厨房的大窗户里透出来的灯光让我明白E1公寓遮挡他家的阳光已经达到白天也需要开灯的程度。对此我感到很羞愧。不过，他家厨房里那张白色的餐桌和悬挂在其正上方的灯看起来既舒适又吸引人。我很快就能坐在那里了，就在尤金的对面，我要告诉他我的卧室就在他家上面。我应该会告诉他的。

在接下来的三十分钟内我换好了衣服，涂了一点儿粉红色的唇膏，并且拿好了我的课本。然后我进去告诉母亲我要去一位朋友家温习功课。我没有预料到她的反应。

"你今天要外出？"她提到"今天"这个字眼的声音好像是在警告我暴风雨即将来临。她完全不相信自己听到的。我还没来得及开口说话，只见她已经向我走来，在我伸手拿书的同时她一把抓住了我的胳膊肘。

“女儿，总统被杀害了。他是一个伟大的人，我们必须表示对他的敬意。今天晚上和我一起去教堂吧。”

她试图拥抱我，但是我的课本挡住了她。我的第一反应是去安慰她，因为她看起来心烦意乱，但是我必须在十五分钟内赶到尤金家。

“我要复习考试，妈妈。八点钟之前我一定会回家。”

“你忘了自己是谁，妮娜。我曾看到你盯着下面那个男孩家的房子发呆。你在把自己推向屈辱和痛苦的深渊。”母亲操着西班牙语用一种听天由命的口吻说道，好像她根本无意阻止我走向“屈辱和痛苦的深渊”，对此我感到很吃惊。我向门口走去。她坐在电视机前，用一条洁白的手帕捂住了脸。

我走到街上，绕过将E1公寓和尤金家隔开的铁丝网栅栏。尤金家院子里的草坪沿着一条通向房子大门的小径被打理得整整齐齐。让我感到诧异的是为什么帕特森市中心位置的建筑都没有得到合理的规划，像尤金家这样小巧整洁的独立住宅旁总是可以找到一座像E1公寓那样庞大破旧的公寓楼。我猜是这些小房子建成在先，为了容纳后来蜂拥而至的移民——先是意大利人、爱尔兰人、犹太人，后来是我们波多黎各人和黑人，这些丑陋的高楼就接二连三地冒了出来。尤金家的大门被漆成了深绿色。绿色是希望的颜色。我曾经听母亲用西班牙语说到这个词：绿色的希望。

我轻轻地敲了敲门。紧张不安地等待片刻之后，门打开了一条小缝，后面出现一张白里透红，略微浮肿的女人的脸。只见一头红色的秀发飘在她那张标致的乳白色的娃娃脸上，鼻子上还有些雀斑。她浓重的眼妆已经花了，看起来像变形橱窗里的模特儿，一点儿也不真实。

“你有什么事？”她的声音很小，但是听起来很悦耳，就像个小女孩的声音，但是她的语气却不那么友好。

“我是尤金的朋友，是他让我过来的。来温习功课。”我把书推给她看。这个愚蠢的动作马上让我觉得窘迫极了。

“你住在那里？”她用手指了指E1公寓。此时看过去，E1公寓显得尤其丑陋，就像一座灰色的监狱，窗户肮脏不堪，消防梯锈迹斑斑。此时，这个女人已经探出半个身子，我看到她穿着一身白色的护士服，名字标签上写着“圣约瑟夫医院”字样。

“是的，我住在那里。”

她目不转睛地看了我一会儿，有点儿像自言自语地说道：“我真不知道你们这些人怎么在那里住得下去。”然后直接对我说道：“听着，亲爱的，尤金并不想和你一起复习功课。他是一个聪明的男孩，不需要任何帮助。你应该明白我的意思吧。如果真是他让你过来的话，我感到非常抱歉。他不能和你一块儿学习。我并不是针对你，你明白吗？我们不会在这个地方待很久的，所以他没有必要和这里的人走得太近——这只会让他日后更难过。赶紧跑回家去吧。”

我一步也没有动。我没有想到那样甜蜜的声音竟然会说出这么一番话，我完全惊呆了。除了尤金之外，我从来没有听到过那么悦耳的声音。她说话的时候就好像在向我唱一支动听的小曲儿。

“你是怎么回事？难道没有听到我的话吗？”她看起来非常生气。我最终从恍惚之中清醒过来。我转身离开这扇绿色的大门，听到门在我身后被轻轻地关上了。

我回到家中，发现家里空无一人。我母亲在别人家的厨房里寻求她需要的安慰。父亲上完晚班以后才能赶回家。那天晚上，我听到他们在厨房轻声地谈了几个小时。这次，他们没有像往常一样谈论他们将来的梦想，或者他们在波多黎各的生活；他们会伤心地谈论总统年轻的遗孀和他们的一双儿女，就好像他们是一家人一样。在接下来的几天，我们会在公寓里进行哀悼，也就是说我们要克制自己，保持沉默——不能听音乐，也不能有笑声。E1公寓的一些妇女还将一连几周都穿着黑色的外套。

那个晚上，我躺在自己的床上，试图为我们逝去的总统感到悲伤和难过，但流出的眼泪却分明是在为自己的遭遇而难过，而不是为我们逝去的总统。母亲来到我门口的时候，我假装自己已经睡着了。夜里的某个时候，我从床上看到外面的路灯亮了起来，氤氲着一圈粉色的光晕。我走向窗台，将脸贴靠在冰冷的玻璃上。抬头仰视灯光的时候，我看到洁白的雪花纷纷扬扬地洒落下来，就好像给天空蒙上了一层美丽的蕾丝面纱。我没有向下看，因为我知道一旦落到地面，这些洁白的雪花就会变成灰色的泥浆。

American History

My ninth grade class had been out in the fenced, playground of Public School Number 13. We had been given "free" exercise time and had been ordered by our P.E. teacher, Mr. DePalma, to "keep moving." That meant that the girls should jump rope and the boys toss basketballs through a hoop at the far end of the yard. He in the meantime would "keep an eye" on us from just inside the building.

It was a cold gray day in Paterson. The kind that warns of early snow. I was miserable, since I had forgotten my gloves and my knuckles were turning red and raw from the jump rope. I was also taking a lot of abuse from the black girls for not turning the rope hard and fast enough for them.

"Hey, Skinny Bones, pump it, girl. Ain't you got no energy today?" Gail, the biggest of the black girls who had the other end of the rope, yelled, "Didn't you eat your rice and beans and pork chops for breakfast today?"

The other girls picked up the "pork chop" and made it into a refrain: "Pork chop, pork chop, did you eat your pork chop?" They entered the double ropes in pairs and exited without tripping or missing a beat. I felt a burning on my cheeks, and then my glasses fogged up so that I could not manage to coordinate the jump rope with Gail. The chill was doing to me what it always did, entering my bones, making me cry, humiliating me. I hated the city, especially in winter. I hated Public School Number 13. I hated my skinny flat-chested body, and I envied the black girls who could jump rope so fast that their legs became a blur. They always seemed to be warm while I froze.

There was only one source of beauty and light for me that school year. The only thing I had anticipated at the start of the semester. That was seeing Eugene. In August, Eugene and his family had moved into the only house on the block that had a yard and trees. I could see his place from my window in El Building. In fact, if I sat on the fire escape I was literally suspended above Eugene's backyard. It was my favorite spot to read my library books in the summer. Until that August the house had been occupied by an old Jewish couple. Over the years I had become part of their family, without their knowing it, of course. I had a view of their kitchen and their backyard, and though I could not hear what they said, I knew when they were arguing, when one of them was sick, and many other things. I knew all this by watching them at mealtimes. I could see their kitchen table, the sink, and the stove. During good times, he sat at the table and read his newspapers while she fixed the meals. If they argued, he would leave and the old woman would sit and stare at nothing for a long time. When one of them was sick, the other would come and get things from the kitchen and carry them out on a tray. The old man had died in June. The last week of school I had not seen him at the table at all. Then one day I saw that there was a crowd in the kitchen. The old woman had finally emerged from the house on the arm of a stocky middle-aged woman whom I had seen there a few times before, maybe her daughter. Then a man had carried out suitcases. The house had stood empty for weeks. I had had to resist the temptation to climb down into the yard and water the flowers the old lady had taken such good care of.

By the time Eugene's family moved in, the yard was a tangled mass of weeds. The father had spent several days mowing, and when he finished, I didn't see the red, yellow, and purple clusters that meant flowers to me from where I sat. I didn't see this family sit down at the kitchen table together. It was just the mother, a red-headed tall woman who wore a white, uniform—a nurse's, I guessed it was; the father was gone before I got up in the morning and was never there at dinner time. I only saw him on weekends when they sometimes sat on lawn chairs under the oak tree, each hidden behind a section of the newspaper; and there was Eugene. He was tall and blond, and he wore glasses. I liked him right away because he sat at the kitchen table and read books for hours. That summer, before we had even spoken one word to each other, I kept him company on my fire escape.

Once school started I looked for him in all my classes, but P.S. 13 was a huge, overpopulated place and it took me days and many discreet questions to discover that Eugene was in honors classes for all his subjects; classes that were not open to me because English was not my first language, though I was a straight A student. After much maneuvering I managed "to run into him" in the hallway where his locker was—on the other side of the building from mine—and in study hall at the library, where he first seemed, to notice me but did not speak; and finally, on the way home after school one day when I decided to approach him directly, though my stomach was doing somersaults.

I was ready for rejection, snobbery, the worst. But when I came up to him, practically panting in my nervousness, and blurted out: "You're Eugene. Right?" He smiled, pushed his glasses up on his nose, and nodded. I saw then that he was blushing deeply. Eugene liked me, but he was shy. I did most of the talking that day. He nodded and smiled a lot. In the weeks that followed, we walked home together. He would linger at the corner of El Building for a few minutes then walk down to his two-story house. It was not until Eugene moved into that house that I noticed that El Building blocked most of the sun and that the only spot that got a little sunlight during the day was the tiny square of earth the old woman had planted with flowers.

I did not tell Eugene that I could see inside his kitchen from my bedroom. I felt dishonest, but I liked my secret sharing of his evenings, especially now that I knew what he was reading, since we chose our books together at the school library.

One day my mother came into my room as I was sitting on the windowsill staring out. In her abrupt way she said: "Elena, you are acting 'moony.' " Enamorada was what she really said—that is, like a girl stupidly infatuated. Since I had turned fourteen and started menstruating my mother had been more vigilant than ever. She acted as if I was going to go crazy or explode or something if she didn't watch me and nag me all the time about being a senorita now. She kept talking about virtue, morality, and other subjects that did not interest me in the least. My mother was unhappy in Paterson, but my father had a good job at the blue jeans factory in Passaic, and soon, he kept assuring us, we would be moving to our own house there. Every Sunday we drove out to the suburbs of Paterson, Clifton, and Passaic, out to where people mowed grass on Sundays in the summer and where children made snowmen in the winter from pure white snow, not like the gray slush of Paterson, which seemed to fall from the sky in that hue. I had learned to listen to my parents' dreams, which were spoken in Spanish, as fairy tales, like the stories about life in the island paradise of Puerto Rico before I was born. I had been to the Island once as a little girl, to Grand mother's funeral, and all I remembered was wailing women in black, my mother becoming hysterical and being given a pill that made her sleep two days, and I feeling lost in a crowd of strangers all claiming to be my aunts, uncles, and cousins. I had actually been glad to return to the city. We had not been back there since then, though my parents talked constantly about buying a house on the beach someday, retiring on the Island—that was a common topic among the residents of El Building. As for me, I was going to go to college and become a teacher.

But after meeting Eugene I began to think of the present more than of the future. What I wanted now was to enter that house I had watched for so many years. I wanted to see the other rooms where the old people had lived and where the boy I liked spent his time. Most of all, I wanted to sit at the kitchen table with Eugene like two adults, like the old man and his wife had done, maybe drink some coffee and talk about books. I had started reading *Gone With the Wind.* I was enthralled by it, with the daring and the passion of the beautiful girl living in a mansion, and with her devoted parents and the slaves who did everything for them. I didn't believe such a world had ever really existed, and I wanted to ask Eugene some questions, since he and his parents, he had told me, had come up from Georgia, the same place where the novel was set. His father worked for a company that had transferred him to Paterson. His mother was very unhappy, Eugene said, in his beautiful voice that rose and fell over words in a strange, lilting way. The kids at school called him the Hick and made fun of the way he talked. I knew I was his only friend so far, and I liked that, though I felt sad for him sometimes. Skinny Bones and the Hick, was what they called us at school when we were seen together.

The day Mr. DePalma came out into the cold and asked us to line up in front of him was the day that President Kennedy was shot. Mr. DePalma, a short, muscular man with slicked-down black hair, was the science teacher, P.E. coach, and disciplinarian at P.S. 13. He was the teacher to whose homeroom you got assigned if you were a troublemaker, and the man called out to break up playground fights, and to escort violently angry teenagers to the office. And Mr. DePalma was the man who called your parents in for "a conference."

That day, he stood in front of two rows of mostly black and Puerto Rican kids, brittle from their efforts to "keep moving" on a November day that was turning bitter cold. Mr. DePalma, to our complete shock, was crying. Not just silent adult tears, but really sobbing. There were a few titters from the back of the line where I stood, shivering.

"Listen." Mr. DePalma raised his arms over his head as if he were about to conduct an orchestra. His voice broke, and he covered his face with his hands. His barrel chest was heaving. Someone giggled behind me.

"Listen," he repeated, "something awful has happened." A strange gurgling came from his throat, and he turned around and spit on the cement behind him.

"Gross," someone said, and there was a lot of laughter.

"The president is dead, you idiots. I should have known that wouldn't mean anything to a bunch of losers like you kids. Go home." He was shrieking now. No one moved for a minute or two, but then a big girl let out a "yeah!" and ran to get her books piled up with the others against the brick wall of the school building. The others followed in a mad scramble to get their things before somebody caught on. It was still an hour to the dismissal bell.

A little scared, I headed for El Building. There was an eerie feeling on the streets. I looked into Mario's drugstore, a favorite hangout for the high school crowd, but there were only a couple of old Jewish men at the soda bar, talking with the short order cook in tones that sounded almost angry, but they were keeping their voices low. Even the traffic on one of the busiest intersections in Paterson—Straight Street and Park Avenue—seemed to be moving slower. There were no horns blasting that day. At El Building, the usual little group of unemployed men were not hanging out on the front stoop, making it difficult for women to enter the front door.

No music spilled out from open doors in the hallway. When I walked into our apartment, I found my mother sitting in front of the grainy picture of the television set.

She looked up at me with a tear-streaked face and just said: "Dios mio," turning back to the set as if it were pulling at her eyes. I went into my room.

Though I wanted to feel the right thing about President Kennedy's death, I could not fight the feeling of elation that stirred in my chest. Today was the day I was to visit Eugene in his house. He had asked me to come over after school to study for an American history test with him. We had also planned to walk to the public library together. I looked down into his yard. The oak tree was bare of leaves, and the ground looked gray with ice. The light through the large kitchen window of his house told me that El Building blocked the sun to such an extent that they had to turn lights on in the middle of the day. I felt ashamed about it. But the white kitchen table with the lamp hanging just above it looked cozy and inviting. I would soon sit there, across from Eugene, and I would tell him about my perch just above his house. Maybe I would.

In the next thirty minutes I changed clothes, put on a little pink lipstick, and got my books together. Then I went in to tell my mother that I was going to a friend's house to study. I did not expect her reaction.

"You are going out today?" The way she said "today" sounded as if a storm warning had been issued. It was said in utter disbelief. Before I could answer, she came toward me and held my elbows as I clutched my books.

"Hija, the president has been killed. We must show respect. He was a great man. Come to church with me tonight."

She tried to embrace me, but my books were in the way. My first impulse was to comfort her, she seemed so distraught, but I had to meet Eugene in fifteen minutes.

"I have a test to study for, Mama. I will be home by eight."

"You are forgetting who you are, Nina. I have seen you staring down at that boy's house. You are heading for humiliation and pain." My mother said this in Spanish and in a resigned tone that surprised me, as if she had no intention of stopping me from "heading for humiliation and pain." I started for the door. She sat in front of the TV, holding a white handkerchief to her face.

I walked out to the street and around the chain-link fence that separated El Building from Eugene's house. The yard was neatly edged around the little walk that led to the door. It always amazed me how Paterson, the inner core of the city, had no apparent logic to its architecture. Small, neat, single residences like this one could be found right next to huge, dilapidated apartment buildings like El Building. My guess was that the little houses had been there first, then the immigrants had come in droves, and the monstrosities had been raised for them—the Italians, the Irish, the Jews, and now us, the Puerto Ricans, and the blacks. The door was painted a deep green: verde, the color of hope. I had heard my mother say it: Verde-Esperanza.

I knocked softly. A few suspenseful moments later the door opened just a crack. The red, swollen face of a woman appeared. She had a halo of red hair floating over a delicate ivory face—the face of a doll—with freckles on the nose. Her smudged eye makeup made her look unreal to me, like a mannequin seen through a warped store window.

"What do you want?" Her voice was tiny and sweet-sounding, like a little girl's, but her tone was not friendly.

"I'm Eugene's friend. He asked me over. To study." I thrust out my books, a silly gesture that embarrassed me almost immediately.

"You live there?" She pointed up to El Building, which looked particularly ugly, like a gray prison with its many dirty windows and rusty fire escapes. The woman had stepped halfway out, and I could see that she wore a white nurse's uniform with "St. Joseph's Hospital" on the name tag.

"Yes. I do."

She looked intently at me for a couple of heartbeats, then said as if to herself, "I don't know how you people do it." Then directly to me. "Listen, Honey, Eugene doesn't want to study with you. He is a smart boy. Doesn't need help. You understand me. I am truly sorry if he told you could come over. He cannot study with you. It's nothing personal. You understand? We won't be in this place much longer, no need for him to get close to people—it'll just make it harder for him later. Run back home now."

I couldn't move. I just stood there in shock at hearing these things said to me in such a honey-drenched voice. I had never heard an accent like hers except for Eugene's softer version. It was as if she were singing me a little song.

"What's wrong? Didn't you hear what I said." She seemed very angry, and I finally snapped out of my trance. I turned away from the green door and heard her close it gently.

Our apartment was empty when I got home. My mother was in someone else's kitchen, seeking the solace she needed. Father would come in from his late shift at midnight. I would hear them talking softly in the kitchen for hours that night. They would not discuss their dreams for the future, or life in Puerto Rico, as they often did; that night they would talk sadly about the young widow and her two children, as if they were family. For the next few days, we would observe luto in our apartment; that is, we would practice restraint and silence—no loud music or laughter. Some of the women of El Building would wear black for weeks.

That night, I lay in my bed, trying to feel the right thing for our dead president. But the tears that came up from a deep source inside me were strictly for me. When my mother came to the door; I pretended to be sleeping. Sometime during the night, I saw from my bed the streetlight come on. It had a pink halo around it. I went to my window and pressed my face to the cool glass. Looking up at the light I could see the white snow falling like a lace veil over its face. I did not look down to see it turning gray as it touched the ground below.

到乡下去
Going to Countryside

尽管才早上八点钟，温度计上的刻度已经急速上升到八十华氏度。我的母亲已经把我和我的弟弟基兰送上了从我的家乡纽约开往北卡罗林那叔叔婶婶家的南行客车上。她在一家制衣厂找到了一份新的工作，这份工作有望让我们过上更好的生活。但是她是晚上上班，这样一来当她出去工作的时候，就没有人照顾我和弟弟。为了安全起见，她决定把我和弟弟基兰送上从我的家乡纽约开往北卡罗林那叔叔婶婶家的南行客车上。以前我从来没有离开过纽约，所以对于出远门，我感到很紧张，更何况我还没见过叔叔婶婶呢。

“埃希，现在你们要有最好的表现，尊敬你的长辈和照顾好弟弟，听到了吗？”她是在告诫我，但是我在她的眼角处分明看到了泪水。我知道在接下来的三个月里她肯定会想念我们。她静静地站在那儿，挥手向我们道别，直到她的柠檬黄裙子在远处变成了一个小点。

基兰和我已经应允好彼此留意旅途中所有与纽约城不同的东西。透过车窗徐徐吹进的微风，减轻了车内炎热的程度。我们把鼻子贴在车窗上，看到密集的错综复杂的建筑物慢慢变得稀少，然后渐渐消失，当我们到达不熟悉的南方农场时，一栋这样的建筑也看不到了。我们嚼着母亲为我们打包的腌制泡菜和黄油三明治，从白软面包吐司中吸着橘子酱，看着绿草地疾驰而过。

德斯蒙德叔叔在车站迎接我们，他是一个沉默寡言的男人，由于长时间在太阳下工作，皮肤被晒得黝黑。他带我们回到他整洁的带着红色谷仓的白房子的路上，几乎一句话也没说。他的房子和母亲向我们描述的以及我小时候在书上看到的图画没有什么区别。第一眼看上去，米勒婶婶和我的母亲真是天壤之别，我的母亲线条清晰，棱角分明，而她五官模糊，头发松散，臀部圆润。她那张和善的脸和精明的眼神显得格外睿智。她看了看我们城里人的这身打扮，说道：

“我会去看看有没有你们的堂兄穿旧的你们能穿的衣服，你们也不想磨损这身漂亮的衣服吧。但精致的衣服和名牌皮鞋在农场并不适用，而且你们俩在这儿肯定是要做点儿事情的。现在你们堂兄埃克将会带你们去清洗一下，然后我们吃晚饭。”

在农场里吃第一餐之前，我从没有看到过那么丰盛的晚餐。紫甘蓝、红眼肉汁曲奇饼干、炸鸡、通心粉和芝士。这些大部分我在家都吃过，但这些食物尝起来有种不同的味道，让人很难下筷。尽管它们是来自其他地方，而不是神奇地出现在餐桌上，但尝起来有种农场的味道——动物和泥土的味儿。我瞥了一眼基兰，他已经狼吞虎咽地吃了起来。

第二天，基兰和我早早就被米勒婶婶叫醒了，她拿来两件可能是埃克穿旧的罩衣，让我们穿上。埃克和德斯蒙德叔叔早就起床了，手里提着几桶热牛奶走了过来，其中一部分会留在农场自己食用，剩下的大部分则会先被储存起来，然后被佛吉尼亚一个芝士工厂收购走去制作芝士。

然后埃克教我们怎样从鸡舍收集鸡蛋，这很快就成为那一整个夏天我最喜爱的工作。我喜欢在黎明前出门，那时的空气还是凉爽潮湿的，我光着脚丫子踩在被露水打湿的草地上，感觉好极了。我小心翼翼地走近鸡笼旁，以免打扰正在酣睡的母鸡。一路上，我一直担心自己快速移动的脚步声和不小心产生的噪声会惊动它们。然后，我伸出无限温柔的手向母鸡柔软的羽毛下面摸去，我能感受到它们的呼吸、它们身上的温度。最后终于摸到了光滑滑的鸡蛋，我小心翼翼地将鸡蛋一个个捡起来放进篮子里。

晚上我会洗个澡，米勒婶婶会放下她晚上的农活帮我梳辫子。但是与母亲帮我辫的复杂的样式相反，米勒婶婶只会辫松散的辫子，甚至有时仅仅把它们辫成一个马尾，任其在我的脖子上轻轻移动。有时候，当米勒婶婶高兴的时候，她会拿鸡蛋黄和牛奶轻轻涂在一股股发束上，将这种混合物一直梳到发根。随后我会高兴地看到我那脆弱卷曲的头发竟然变得柔软起来。

经过大量户外运动后，我的四肢变得灵活起来。我发现基兰由于天天在牧场上与埃克一起奔跑也变得更加强壮。下午太热而无法做任何事的时候，我们会躺在巨大橡树的树荫下，咀嚼着青草，在甜美、绿色的味道以及自己的梦里迷失。

Going to Countryside

Even at eight in the morning, the thermometer was heading up towards 80 degrees when my mother put me and my brother Kiran on the southbound bus heading from our home in New Youk City to our aunt and uncle's place in North Carolina. Her new job on the third shift of the garment factory gave us the potential for a better life ahead, but she was wary about leaving us alone at home in the evenings and overnight. I had never been outside of New York City before, so I was nervous about moving, not to mention that I had never met my aunt and uncle before.

"Now Essie, you be on your best behavior, mind your elders and watch out for your little brother, you hear me?" Her words were admonishments, but I saw the tear in the corner of her eye and knew that she'd miss us over the next three months. She stood still, arm upraised in farewell, until her lemon-yellow dress became no more than a pinprick in the distance.

Kiran and I had promised each other that we would notice all the things that were different from New York while we were on our trip. In the bus, the heat of the road was balanced to some degree by the breeze blowing in through the windows. We pressed our noses up to the glass, peering out as the dense thicket of buildings thinned, then disappeared altogether as we hit the unfamiliar farm country in the South. We chewed the soggy pickle and butter sandwiches our mother had packed for us, sucking the juice from between the slices of white, soft bread and watched the green fields rush by.

We were greeted at the bus station by Uncle Desmond, a quiet man whose skin shone dark from working out in the sun. He said almost nothing as he took us back to his neat white house with its red barn that looked just like my mother's descriptions of it and the pictures in books I'd seen when I was younger. At first glance, Aunt Millie seemed the polar opposite of my mother. Where my mother was all sharp lines and tight angles, Aunt Millie was almost blurred, her hair looser and her hips more ample. Still, her kind face and shrewd glance at our city outfits showed the same deep intelligence.

"We're gonna have to see if some of your cousin's old overalls can be taken up for you. Don't want to get your nice things scuffed up. Farm life's not easy on fancy dresses and patent leather shoes and you'll both be doing your share of the chores around here, that's for sure! Now your cousin Ike'll show you where to go to get washed up for dinner."

I had never seen so much food in my life before that first meal at the farm. Collard greens, biscuits with red-eye gravy, fried chicken, macaroni and cheese—I'd eaten most of these dishes at home, but here they tasted different in a way that was hard to put a finger on at first. As though they were from somewhere, instead of appearing magically on our kitchen table. They tasted the way the farm smelled—of the animals and the earth. I glanced over at Kiran, and he was digging in hungrily.

The next day, Kiran and I were roused early by Aunt Millie carrying two smaller versions of what, presumably, had been Ike's old overalls. Ike and Desmond, who had both been awake hours earlier, came by carrying pails of warm milk, some of which would be put to household use while the main load was put by to be picked up by a cheese-making facility in Virginia.

Ike then taught us to gather eggs from the chickens in the henhouse. This quickly became my favorite task over that summer. I loved going out into the early dawn, the air still cool and damp and feeling my bare feet sink into grass wet with dew. I'd approach the coop with great care not to disturb the slumbering ladies, as I thought of them, making sure not to betray my presence by any quick movement or careless noise. Then, with infinite gentleness, I'd reach out, my hands rustling under the soft feathers of the hens, sensing their respiration, their warmth, feeling for the smooth white eggs and placing each one I found carefully into my basket.

At night I would take a bath and Aunt Millie would take time away from her evening chores to braid my hair. But instead of the intricate patterns my mother liked to make, Aunt Millie gave me looser plaits and even sometimes gathered them into a single tail inching down my neck. Sometimes, when Aunt Millie seemed in an especially good mood, we would condition it with egg yolk and milk, which Aunt Millie would work into my hair gently massaging each strand, working the mixture deep into the roots. Afterwards I was pleased to see how the brittle, frizzy ends softened.

My body became loose-limbed from the outdoor exercise and I noticed Kiran growing stronger and bolder as he ran through the fields with Ike. In the afternoons when it was too hot to do anything else, we'd lie in the shade of the huge oak tree, chewing on grass stems, lost in the sweet, green taste and our own thoughts.

我的钢琴老师
My Piano Teacher

玛丽安·林登在第九大道北面一套一室公寓里教授钢琴。公寓虽然狭小，却被收拾得一尘不染。不知道出于什么原因，她竟然同意以低于其他人的收费标准来教我弹钢琴。那年夏天我已年满十二周岁。在去玛丽安·林登家学钢琴之前，因为不愿意去上黑泽尔小姐的钢琴课，我已经和爸爸斗争好几个月了。让我感到非常奇怪的一点是，在我告诉他黑泽尔小姐因为我犯一点点小错就用尺子打我的手指后，他竟然都无动于衷。我猜可能是因为价格的问题。他依然坚持送葛丽塔去那里学免费的钢琴课，但是我最终还是拒绝了。僵持了数月后，爸爸突然开始不断提到玛丽安·林登这个名字，好像他对她特别了解。住在小镇北部的某位音乐天才要举办一场钢琴独奏会。当地报纸对此事进行了报道，而林登小姐作为他的指导老师，照片也上了报。或许是林登小姐的照片让爸爸想起了他的姐姐梅布尔。抑或爸爸急于找到一个比黑泽尔小姐更有说服力的人，能让我不吵不闹地坐在钢琴前，这样总算完成了妈妈的一个心愿。当他开始提到憧憬着我在卡内基音乐大厅的首演的时候，他一定已经意识到要实现这个梦想应该从上课开始。他没有给林登小姐打电话，因为过去的经验让他明白，什么都不如面对面的交流让人印象深刻。所以，在一个周六他把我拽上车，厚着脸皮来到了林登小姐的门前。林登小姐住的公寓离我的住处有八千米的距离。

我对林登小姐心生敬畏，一时也忘了对爸爸如此唐突之举的愠怒。她待人谦和宽厚，热情地邀请我们进入她的客厅，甚至请我们喝茶。我直挺挺地坐在靠背椅上，听爸爸和林登小姐谈话。爸爸平静地谈到了妈妈的去世，我根本没有的音乐才华以及他对我的期望。他还顺带提了下他名下数百万美元的财产以及伐木权——当时至少有五家大型的木材公司在激烈地竞争这个伐木权。林登小姐耐心地听着爸爸的讲述。在恰当的时候，她会吸口气，随声附和句："我明白。"她的反应着实让人难以理解。她那与生俱来的高贵的气质让她显得很有自制力。她年纪并不大，却处处显得持重自爱，尊重别人。她琥珀色的浓密秀发开始有些灰白。她把头发往上梳成弓形，上面别着一把龟甲做的梳子。

爸爸还在喋喋不休地讲着，我趁机会环顾了下这座小公寓。四周的墙壁是简单朴实的白色。离我们稍远的窗户边放着一架施坦威钢琴，泛着圆润的光泽。房间的中央铺着一小块充满东方风情的地毯。白色的墙面上挂着几幅精心挑选的画，画与画之间的距离均衡得恰到好处。最后，她同意暂时收下我，并且费用优惠。我至今都不明白她做这个决定是因为她天性善良还是出于对我的同情。这次见面和租间房子或者被埃奇蒙特学校录取没有什么区别。爸爸对这件事的促成，让我感觉是通过欺骗手段实现的。关于这一点，我内心斗争得很厉害。一个声音说："我们不得不承认，他说的大部分都是真实的，难道不是吗？"另一个声音说："是的，大部分是事实。但是，为了达到目的，事实在一定程度上也可以被操作和利用，这样的做法几乎等同于说谎了。更何况，关于金矿和数百万美元财产的事不是真的，完全是爸爸臆想出来的。"接着，我自己也糊涂了，如果这些是凭空想象出来的，那我们靠什么生活呢？最后，我决定相信它们，但同时保持着质疑的态度。怀疑其实就相当于不相信，没有任何风险地不相信。

就这样，我每周一次在放学后搭乘公共汽车来到这座黑色砖砌建筑物前，看着那些铅框的窗户，爬几层楼梯来到林登小姐的公寓。她从来不对我的未来做无谓的设想，只是要求我把刚学到的技巧练习到最好。大约三周后，她发现有什么事情妨碍我实现这个目标。于是，她尝试用一种柔和且礼貌的方法找出其中的原因。我想承认是因为家里太吵了，我根本没有办法集中精力练习钢琴，又担心这样来会招来更多的警察局女监护。如果再有一次这样的抱怨，他们调查情况后肯定会发现爸爸的精神越来越不正常，从而把我们从家里带走。我不能解释这个问题。对于我来说，现在的钢琴课更多的是种感情上的寄托，而不是一个学习目标。我很担心如果我一直没有什么进步，林登小姐会停止教授我钢琴；但是我也想不出办法克服影响我进步的内心混乱。每周能有那么一天可以安静地坐在钢琴凳上，感觉到她在我的身边，关心着我，而我也知道她在做什么，对我来说已经足够了。能够待在她家里，通过墙上的画，还有她的一举一动，感知艺术、真实和文明的气息，我还能奢求什么呢？可惜，我一直没有找到合适的方法把这些表达给她听。

My Piano Teacher

Marian Linden taught piano in a small, immaculate studio apartment on 9th Avenue North. For some reason that I will never understand, she agreed to take me as a pupil at a reduced rate the summer I turned twelve. I had fought with Daddy for months over my lessons with Hazel. Even when I told him that she hit my fingers with a ruler when I made mistakes, he was curiously undisturbed; I guess the price was right. He continued sending Greta to her free of charge, but I finally refused. After a standoff of many months, he started to throw Marian Linden's name around as though he'd known her all his life. Some prodigy who lived in the north end of town had given a recital that was covered by the local papers, and Miss Linden's picture had been featured as his teacher. Maybe she remained Daddy of his sister, Mabel. Maybe he was just desperate to find someone more impressive than Hazel who could keep me at the keyboard with a minimum of strife, and thus fulfill another one of Mother's dreams. By the time he'd begun alluding to my Carnegie Hall debut, he must have realized it would help to start with lessons. He didn't phone Miss Linden because he had learned from experience that nothing beat a face-to-face encounter; he simply forced me into the car one Saturday and brazened it out at her door five miles later.

I was too awed by her to sulk. She was very gracious, inviting us into her living room and even offering tea. I sat stiffly in a straight–backed chair and listened as Daddy calmly cited Mother's death, my nonexistent talent, his great dreams for me and incidentally, the multimillion–dollar property in his name, the timber rights to which at this very moment no less than five major lumber companies were turning purple competing for. Marian Linden listened politely, drew in her breath at the appropriate moments, and said, "I see." It was hard to interpret her reactions; she had an innate dignity that made her seem very well–contained. She was not an old woman, but she carried herself with a certain respect and treated others that way, too. Her amber hair was thick, and just beginning to gray. She wore it in an upswept style, held in place with a large tortoise–shell comb.

As Daddy's voice droned on, I let my eyes wander around the apartment. The walls were a stark white and the Steinway glistened richly at the far end of the room, by the window. There was a small Oriental rug in the middle of the room, and well–chose prints hung at balanced intervals along the white walls. By the end of our visit, she had agreed to take me on provisionally, at the reduced fee. I don't know whether it was kindness or pity that motivated her and I have trouble making that distinction even to this day. The interview felt no different from renting the homes, or being enrolled in the Edgemont School: After watching him operate, I always felt I had gained admission by fraudulent means. I would argue this point with myself, saying: Well most of what he said was true, wasn't it? And I'd answer, yes, it was true, but there are certain uses to which the truth can be put, certain ways of manipulating it, that come dangerously close to lying. The gold mines and properties weren't true; those were just figments of his imagination. But then I'd get confused; because if those weren't true, then how would we survive? I ended up believing in them, while at the same time retaining my skepticism about them—which amounted to a form of nonbelief, without the risk.

Once a week I took the bus after school to the dark brick building with the leaded windows and climbed the stairs to Miss Linden's apartment. She had no delusions about my future, only a steady belief in the perfectibility of present skills. It took her about three weeks to see that something was standing in my way of achieving that goal. She tried, in a gentle and respectful way, to find out what was wrong. I was torn between the wish to confess the chaos at home and its effects on my concentration, and the fear of more Police Department matrons if I did.Investigating a second complaint, they would be sure to notice Daddy's growing disintegration and remove us from the home. I couldn't explain that, for me, the lessons had become less a goal than an emotional oasis. I was terrified that she would terminate them because of my lack of progress, yet could think of no way to overcome the turmoil inside that kept me from progressing. It was enough just to be in her presence each week, to slide onto the piano bench and feel her there at my side, concerned, and knowing what she was doing. It was enough to see the evidence of art and truth and civilization there on her walls, and in her gestures. I groped for some way to get this across to her, but failed.

音乐的力量
The Power of Music

我过去写歌常常会感到痛苦。

通常，创作的灵感来自得到或失去一个女孩。当我的心痛达到一种笨拙的抑郁状态的时候，语言和曲调结合到一起演奏出来时对悲伤的缓解，犹如飘落的雨滴对沉重乌云的释放。我认为我们大多数人写歌都是宣泄内心的情感，抑制不说话不利于身心健康。把它们堵在嘴边，它们会像细菌一样感染。把它们隐藏在歌里，你会突然有一个情感存储仓，这一情感存储仓可以起到净化内心世界的作用。

我们写的第一首歌都是夸张意识流情感的表达。我们创作的主题歌曲往往倾轧着活生生的真人，我们胡乱地编写的嘲弄小夜曲常常烦扰我们的兄弟姐妹，我们用随意的曲调叙述我们内在的生命。作为备受折磨的听众，我们的朋友、熟人或家庭成员会对我们大喊大叫要求我们停止持续不断的噪声。虽然许多掌握了礼貌待人礼节规则的人会学着独享自己的音乐，但作曲家显然做不到这一点。相反，我们会把歌曲变成大家都爱听的东西。

音乐会莫名其妙地让人们完全不羞于表达。在演说中，一个戏剧性地抱怨世界对他不公的人很可能会因缺乏自控力而受到大家的指责。然而在一首歌中，作曲家痛苦的宣泄会被看作一位英雄企图克服困难，从而被接受。歌曲会大胆地宣泄一个人的内心世界。为什么人们会想要进入另一个人的情感世界呢？

在我们享受的音乐里存在两种相反力量的平衡。一种力量平静缓和，另一种则骚动不安。当音乐演奏时，单个音符的实际频率会持续地以不同的数学关系互相衬托。当它们比例均衡时，我们会听到和弦，和声和齐奏。歌曲正常情况下都会以这种关系结束，因为它传达着结束、完成和决心。其他的组合创造出紧张、不适和期待。成功的歌曲就像成功的故事能够赢得听众的心。它们通常先介绍主角，然后带领听众去经历他们的挫败与胜利。甚至多乐章器乐曲也会先介绍一个主旋律，然后通过不同的音乐结构篇章去探索它的旅程。

小孩子喜欢听舒缓的摇篮曲以转移焦虑、紧张或进入平和的梦乡。他们吟唱躁动不安的歌曲时会获得极大的喜悦，就像“nenny nenny boo boo”旋律可以被灵活运用于各种嘲讽中。同样，当成年人想放松或心烦意乱的时候，会选择经典音乐、抒情爵士以及轻音乐；当想要表达不敬或反抗时，会选择更刺激的音乐，如朋克乐、说唱和摇滚。

随着年龄的增大，我们对音乐变得更加挑剔。当我们还是小孩子的时候，我们被动地接受和学习、喜欢自己父母的音乐，就像要喜欢他们做的饭一样，这并不是因为自己的家长一定比其他家长更会做饭，但是通过绝对的熟悉，孩子会更偏向于自己的父母做出的东西。同样，一个孩子成长的文化背景会协调他听的品位，使其偏向于某种节奏，乐器，和声和歌曲结构。作为青年人，我们选择音乐就像选择自己的朋友一样。我们会基于他们的服装、政治倾向、心情以及流行度找到与艺术家的共鸣。我们在歌词中寻找自我定义，把歌曲理解成个人感情的表达。尽管我们不是自己钟爱的歌曲的作者，我们视它为表达自我的小饰品，一些向别人揭示自己内心世界重要部分的配饰。当我们与一首歌曲建立了亲密关系后，当我们听到这首歌时会感受到幸福愉快的波浪在内心涌动，我们内心世界的感受也会流露出来。

作为歌曲作者，我们渴求我们写的每一首歌中表达自己内心的感受。但是，有时我们会害怕若明确地表达自己，会剥夺听众借我们的歌曲平静自己的机会。所以我们经常用通用的符号代替具体的细节。在自己内心保留歌词原始意义的同时，冠以歌曲足够的灵活度，以便他人能够从中得到不同的意义。

作为表演者，我们需要明确的一件事是：音乐对我们来说意味着什么。通过对其他艺术家的观察，我们会模仿欢乐与痛苦的表达。不带真实感情的情感内容很容易创作和演奏，然而，就像观众能够区分好与坏的表演一样，听众能够听出来做作的与真实的演奏之间的差异。

The Power of Music

I used to have to feel pain in order to write songs.

Normally, this inspiration took the form of wanting or losing a girl. My heartsickness would reach a state of such unwieldy gloom that words and melodies would coalesce and fall like raindrops to relieve the stress of carrying such a heavy cloud of misery. I think many of us mainly write songs for relief. It's unhealthy to keep swallowing unspoken words. Keep them on the tip of your tongue and they'll fester like bacteria. Stash them all in a song and you suddenly have an emotional storage unit, which un-clutters your inner world.

The first "songs" we ever write are just exaggerated expressions of our stream of consciousness. We create theme songs while jostling with action figures, concoct mocking serenades to annoy our siblings or narrate our inner lives to a random tune. We have all been yelled at by a frustrated audience of our friends, acquaintances, and family members to cease our incessant noise making. While many learn to keep their songs to themselves as they master the rules of polite etiquette, songwriters apparently never learn. Instead, we begin to turn our songs into something people will happy to hear.

Music somehow makes people feel unashamed about being completely expressive. In speech, someone melodramatically complaining about all the injustices of his world would probably be chastised for lacking self-control. However, in song, a proclamation of suffering is received as an almost heroic attempt to overcome adversity. Songs boldly broadcast a description of someone's inner world. Why do people want to tune into someone else's emotional episodes?

There's a balance of two opposing forces that we enjoy in music. One force soothes, the other agitates. As music plays, the actual frequencies of the individual notes are constantly lining up in different mathematical relations to each other. When they are proportional to each other, we hear chords, harmony, and unison. Songs normally end on this sort of relationship because it conveys closure, completion, resolution. Other combinations create a sense of tension, discomfort, and anticipation. Successful songs win over listeners just as successful stories do. They normally introduce a protagonist and take the listener along to experience some of his/her setbacks and triumphs. Even instrumental pieces often introduce a central melody and then explore its travels through different passages of the song's structure.

Young children often enjoy hearing soothing lullabies as a way to be distracted from anxiety or coaxed into a peaceful slumber. They take great pleasure in singing agitating songs, such as the "nenny nenny boo boo" melody that can be customized into any taunt. Similarly, adults have classical, smooth jazz, and easy listening styles of music when they want to be relaxed or distracted, and they have the more provocative extremes of punk, rap, and metal when they want to use music to express irreverence or rebellion.

We become much more selective in our musical tastes as we age. As children, we passively accept and learn to love our parents' music just like we do their cooking. It's not that a parent necessarily cooks "better" than other parents, but through sheer familiarity a child will greatly prefer her parents, cooking to that of others. Similarly, the cultural backdrop of a child's upbringing calibrates her listening tastes to a given set of rhythms, instruments, harmonic scales, and song structures. As adolescents, though, we begin to choose our own songs just as we would choose our friends. We identify with artists based on their dress, their politics, their mood, their popularity. We look to find personal meaning in lyrics and to latch onto songs that seem to broadcast our private thoughts. Despite not being the author of our favorite songs, we wear our songs like trinkets of personal expression, telltale accessories that describe to others important parts of our psychology. When we develop a kinship with a song, we feel waves of euphoria as it plays, the feeling of our inner world radiating out.

As songwriters, we must aspire to this private release in every song we write. However, sometimes we fear that if we express ourselves too specifically, we will deny listeners the opportunity to mold our song into something they can claim as their own. We often replace specific details with general symbols, preserving for ourselves the original meaning of a lyric while infusing it with enough flexibility that someone else can derive a different significance.

The one thing we must be sure of as performers is that a song means something to us. Through observation of other artists, we learn to mimic expressions of joy and anguish. It becomes easy for us to write and perform songs without any genuine attachment to their emotional content. Nevertheless, just as audiences can distinguish between good and bad acting, so too will audience members feel a difference between a contrived and an authentic performance.

历史的窗口
A Window into History

高中时候的某个漫长的夏天，妈妈让我去帮外公研究我们的家谱。好吧，我勉强同意了。一想到研究家谱，我头脑里出现的画面是一连几个小时在满是灰尘和腐烂的盒子里翻资料，听那些我压根不认识的人的故事。“你一定会感到惊讶的，”妈妈保证道，“家族历史会非常有趣的。”

事实上，外公在研究家族历史之外，也希望保存我们的家族记忆。他发现了一个电脑程序，可以用来扫描老照片和信件，这样在它们毁坏之前，就可以被保存下来。外公希望我能帮他连接扫描仪，设置电脑程序。他会编辑文档、发邮件，但从没用过扫描仪。

与我之前想象的整理满是灰尘的箱子不同，我们在外公整洁、明亮的书房里待了很长时间。伴随着扫描仪嗡嗡的运转声，亲人们的珍贵记忆转化成了可以被永久珍藏的数码图片。我一边开心地工作，一边听外公讲故事，一点儿都不觉得无聊。

夏天一天天过去，我逐渐沉迷于亲人们的人生故事。我请外公告诉我，我们扫描的每张照片和信背后的故事。这些故事不仅让我了解了他们，更拉近了我与他们之间的距离。他们也曾像我一样庆祝成功，克服失败，玩恶作剧，参加运动和音乐会。我希望外公能够多给我讲些故事，他不得不拿出更多的东西来满足我的兴趣。他向我展示了一个箱子，里面塞满了各种东西，全被灰尘覆盖着。

通过阅读他们留下来的东西，我觉得像打开了一扇早已逝去的通向他们的世界的窗户。外公又向我展示了一捆泛黄的书信，那是他在二战期间，从前线寄给外婆的信，我甚至能闻到火药味。我翻开曾祖母的食谱，纸张已经变脆，我能想象到她坐在自己一尘不染的厨房里，认真地书写着每一个条目的样子。那些曾经在我的印象里只是一个名字的人，现在都有了生动的面孔和多彩的生活。

新学期要开始了，外公说："其实我自己也可以做这件事，我只是很想和某个人分享。"我非常感谢外公给予我这次与他分享研究家谱的机会。通过整理亲人们的书信和听外公给我讲他们的故事，我也由衷地感谢我的这些亲人，因为正是由于他们才有我的今天。我会好好珍惜这些家族记忆和他们留下的纪念品，希望有一天，我也可以将这些故事讲给我的子孙听。

A Window into History

One very long summer during high school, my mom volunteered me to help Grandpa research our family tree. Great, I thought, imagining hours spent pawing through dusty, rotting boxes and listening to boring stories about people I didn't know. "You'll be surprised," my mom promised. "Family histories can be very interesting."

It turned out Grandpa had more in mind than research, hoping to also preserve our family memories. He'd discovered a computer program that helps digitally scan old pictures and letters to preserve their contents before they crumble from old age. Grandpa wanted me to help him connect the scanner and set up the computer program. He could type documents and send emails but had never used a scanner.

Instead of sorting through dusty boxes as I had imagined, we spent a lot of time in my grandpa's bright, tidy computer room. The scanner hummed happily, turning my relatives' precious memories into permanent digital images. I worked happily while Grandpa shared stories that turned out not to be boring at all.

As the summer progressed, I became obsessed with my relatives' lives. I asked Grandpa to tell the story behind every picture and letter we scanned. The stories helped me not only understand but relate to my relatives.

Like me, they had celebrated achievements, overcome failures, pulled silly pranks, played sports, and attended concerts. I became so hungry for more information that Grandpa needed additional props to keep me satisfied. He showed me a chest filled with random stuff, all covered in dust.

Perusing through their belongings, I felt I was opening a window into the world of my relatives, a world long since gone. Grandpa showed me a bundle of yellowed letters he had sent to Grandma from the front lines of World War Ⅱ, and I could almost smell the gunpowder. I turned the brittle pages of my great-grandmother's recipe book and could envision her sitting in her immaculate kitchen, penning meticulously every entry. All of the people who had been merely names to me now had faces to match and lives lived.

As the new school year approached, Grandpa admitted, "I probably could have done this project myself. I just wanted someone to share it with." I can't think him enough for sharing the experience and making me appreciate the family members who have made me the person I am. I will cherish family memories and mementoes and hope that someday, I will be able to pass them down to my own grandchildren.

新生活的开始

Moving to a New Life

我孤身一人，站在艾尔姆大街和缅因街的拐角，看着父母离开，内心充满了对这座新城市的恐慌。我尽量不让自己的恐惧表现出来，但又控制不住。眼泪还是流了下来，我慌忙跑回属于我的那间新的、冰冷的卧室。

我知道自己这样是在出丑，但又难以控制自己。我是家里唯一的孩子，从来没有离开父母超过30分钟，而现在，我却远离家乡，来到了我的大学，搬进了我的大学宿舍。我们都想对自己的人生负责，但我却从没想到为此要离开父母。每天早上醒来，我再也吃不到妈妈为我准备的早餐牛奶、新鲜的橙汁、松软的煎蛋和香脆的培根。我还要自己去解字谜游戏，再也没有爸爸含蓄的暗示。这感觉就像是我曾经热爱的一切，都从我的生活里撕掉了。你能明白我正在经历的这些吗？

当我趴在枕头上哭的时候，我听到宿舍的门开了。一定是我的新室友，我赶忙擦干泪——不能让新室友以为我是个脆弱的爱哭鬼，这样可太尴尬了！但让我惊讶的是，我听到她哭着跑回了房间。内心充满着好奇，我踮着脚尖小心翼翼地穿过共同休息室走向她的卧室。

我在门口仅仅站了几秒钟，她就发现了。她突然抬起头，因我的出现而表现出的震惊全然写在脸上。“你还好吗？”我轻声问。“对不起……”她不好意思地说，“我以为只有我一个人。你一定会觉得我很孩子气吧，只是，我跟妹妹的关系非常好，刚刚跟她告别……”她边说变转过头去，“这真的是太难适应了。”

“我完全理解。”我说，而且自己也确实是这样感觉的。“或许我们能互相帮助，一起来适应新的大学生活。”

Moving to a New Life

I stand on the corner of Elm Avenue and Main Street by myself, watching my parents walk away and feeling nothing but apprehension about adjusting to this new town. I try not to show the passersby just how scared I really am, but it's not possible. My tears start to flow, and I quickly run to my new, cold bedroom.

I know I am making a complete spectacle of myself, but I can't help it. I am an only child who has never been more than 30 minutes away from her parents, yet here I am, on the other side of the country, moving in to my new college dorm. We all want to take responsibility for our own lives. I just never realized that in order to do so, I would have to leave my family. No longer will I wake up to Mom's Sunday breakfast of non-pasteurized milk and fresh orange juice, fluffy scrambled eggs and crisp bacon. I'll have to tackle the daily crossword puzzle on my own, without Dad's carefully veiled hints. It feels like everything I have ever loved is being ripped away from me. Can anyone understand what I'm going through?

As I lay crying into my pillow, I hear the door to the dorm suite open. It must be one of my roommates. I quickly stop crying—I couldn't stand the embarrassment if she knew her new roommate was an emotional wreck! Much to my surprise, I hear her crying as she runs to her room. Curiosity overwhelming me, I tiptoe through the common room to her still-open door.

I stand in the doorway for merely a second before she reacts. Abruptly, her face jolts up, and her sudden shock at my appearance is clearly written on her face. "Are you okay?" I quietly ask. "I'm sorry," she stammers. "I thought I was alone. I know this must seem very childish to you. I'm just very close to my young sister, and saying goodbye to her just now"... Her sentence trails off as she turns her face away from me. "It's going to be hard to adjust, that's all."

"I completely understand," I say, and I really do. "Maybe we can help each other to get used to this new college life."

夏日三明治俱乐部
The Summer Sandwich Club

在我漫长的教育生涯中，总有那么一些孩子让我毕生难以忘怀，麦克斯就是其中之一。

我第一次见到麦克斯是在三年前的夏天。当时，他和他妈妈凯瑟琳在夏令营开始的第一天出现在营地所在的公园里。跟我简单说声“早上好”后，麦克斯就跑去和那些五六岁的同龄人玩了。他们在接下来的几周里将接受我的辅导。

当他的妈妈返回车里的时候，我立刻就注意到她看起来非常疲倦，好像刚刚跑完一场马拉松比赛。不过当她驱车离去的时候，我就忘了这件事，因为我很快就被三十个笑容可掬的孩子围了起来，他们都是第一次参加夏令营，在我身边叽叽喳喳，兴奋得很。

这真是一个很棒的开始。我和麦克斯一见如故，他像崇拜哥哥那样崇拜我，而我觉得他真是棒极了。但是有件小事让我觉得非常奇怪：每周有那么一两次，麦克斯总会在午饭一个小时后就开始抱怨说自己很饿。夏令营进行到第三周的时候，我觉得自己应该做些什么去弄清楚在麦克斯身上发生了什么状况。一次午餐的时候，我来到他的桌边，问他我能否和他一起吃午餐。他咯咯笑了，“当然可以，杰克。”他大声说道，他觉得能和我共进午餐是件很自豪的事。他的午餐包括一包炸土豆条、一罐汽水和一根巧克力棒。对于一个五岁的孩子来说，这可算不上一顿健康的午餐。我把一半三明治给他的时候，他兴奋得两眼发亮，就好像得到一件很棒的生日礼物。

那天下午，当他的妈妈凯瑟琳来接他的时候，我把凯瑟琳拉到一边，问了她午餐的事情。

“凯瑟琳，麦克斯需要更健康的午餐。”

“杰克，你这么说是什么意思？”她的眼睛望着地面。

“我的意思是麦克斯不能每天都是吃垃圾食品。”

“哦，原来是这件事。对于这个问题，我很抱歉。我每晚都要工作到清晨，几乎连帮他起床穿衣的时间都不能保证。本来他的保姆应该在侍候他睡觉后把午餐准备好，不过我们最近一直在换保姆，所以有时候就忘了午餐的事，结果我不得不在出发前的最后一分钟搞定所有的事情，不过我会尽量保证这样的事不再发生。”

“谁都有可能遇到这种事。我只是想让你知道他午餐都吃了些什么。有那么几天他抱怨很饿，我有些担心，所以想知道是谁在给他准备午餐。那么，明天早上见，凯瑟琳女士。”

接下来的几天，我希望在午餐的时候能够看到麦克斯吃三明治，可结果看到的依然是垃圾食品。我觉得需要做些什么去改变这种状况，至少要保证他在午餐时不要摄入那么多的糖分。

“凯瑟琳。”那天下午麦克斯的妈妈刚下车我就叫住了她。我真不知道该说些什么才好，觉得有些尴尬。“我们需要解决麦克斯的午餐问题。”

“杰克，我知道。只不过我们的房租昨天到期了，我没有……呃……时间去杂货店，”，她的声音越来越小，“眼下我们的生活有些难挨。”

说这些话的时候她看起来很窘迫。我有些后悔跟她再次提及这件事。我告诉她不用再为这件事担心，因为我想到一个好主意。得知了我的计划后，她的脸上浮现出宽慰和感激的表情。之后，她就带着麦克斯回家了。

在剩下来的时间里，我开始跟麦克斯还有他的朋友们分享我的午餐，并且把我们这个小组织命名为“三明治俱乐部”：每天我都会多准备一些三明治，有兴趣尝试的孩子都可以分到一些。每次午餐的时候，麦克斯似乎都根本不在乎我带了什么样的三明治到俱乐部，只是每次临走前，都会冲我笑笑。

夏令营快结束的时候，我收到一封凯瑟琳写来的信，信上说感谢我对她和麦克斯所做的善举。我回信说我非常期待明年“三明治俱乐部”再次聚首，并请她代表我向麦克斯问好。

在接下来的两年中，“三明治俱乐部”都会在夏季每周一到周五的中午定期聚会。再之后，麦克斯和他的妈妈搬到了离爷爷奶奶家较近的地方，我开始和我的同事一起吃午餐。但是，“三明治俱乐部”带给我和孩子们的快乐将永远铭刻在我的记忆中。

The Summer Sandwich Club

Max was one of those kids I know I will remember for the rest of my life. I first met Max three summers ago when he showed up at the park on the first day of camp with his mother Katherine. After a brief good morning, he went off to play with the rest of the five and six year olds who I would be counseling for the next several weeks. As his mother walked back to her car, I couldn't help but notice that she looked as though she had just finished running a marathon; however, that thought left my mind soon after she drove away, as I was surrounded by the smiling faces of thirty brand new campers.

The summer started off great, and Max and I hit it off right away; he looked up to me as an older brother, and I thought he was a great little kid. There were a few things that stuck out in my mind as odd, though, like when he would complain of being hungry an hour or so after lunch at least once or twice a week. By the third week of camp, I decided that it was something I needed to investigate, and during lunch time I went over to his table and asked if I could sit next to him. He giggled and said, "Sure Jake," feeling special that I would want to spend my lunch break with him. His lunch consisted of a bag of potato chips, a can of soda, and a chocolate bar—hardly a healthy meal for a five year old. I offered him half of my sandwich and his eyes lit up like it was his birthday.

That afternoon, when Katherine came to pick Max up from the park, I pulled her aside to discuss the lunch issue.

"Katherine, Maxwell needs to have a healthy lunch." She looked down at the ground.

"What do you mean, Jake? "

"I mean Max can not keep eating junk food every day."

"Oh. That. I'm sorry about that. It's just that I work back-to-back jobs every night and barely make it home in time to get him out of bed and dressed before camp starts in the moring. His babysitter is supposed to pack Max's lunch for him at night when she puts him to bed. We have had a couple of new babysitters lately, and sometimes they forget to do it, so I end up having to throw something together at the last minute. I'll make sure it doesn't happen any more."

"It happens to the best of us; I just wanted to make sure you knew what he was eating. After a couple days of him being hungry I got worried and wondered who was making his lunch for him. See you tomorrow morning then."

Several days later I expected to see Max eating a sandwich when I went over to him at lunchtime. His lunch once again consisted entirely of junk food. Something had to change; at the very least he needed to be eating much less sugar.

"Katherine," I called to his mother as she stepped out of her car that afternoon. I really had no idea what I was supposed to say. It was quite a predicament. “We really need to fix this problem with Max’s lunch.”

“Jake, I know, it’s just that the house payment was due yesterday, and I haven’t had the, uh, time to get to the grocery store，” she trailed off. “Things are just a little hard for us right now.”

She was obviously self-conscious at the moment, and I felt bad for having brought it up again. I told her that I had a plan, and not to worry about it. After explaining what I meant, the look on her face was one of relief and thanks, and she and Max headed home for the day.

For the rest of the summer, I spent my lunches with Max and his friends, having meetings of what we called the “Sandwich Club”: every day I would bring a couple of extra sandwiches, and anybody who wanted to try one could have some. Max never seemed to care what kind of Sandwich I brought to the club, but just giggled and smiled up at me every afternoon.

At the end of the summer, I got a letter from Katherine, thanking me for being so kind to she and Max. I wrote back telling her that I could hardly wait until the next meeting of the “Sandwich Club ,” and to tell Max that I said hello.

For the next two years, the “Sandwich Club” had regular meetings, Monday—Friday at noon, all summer long. After that, Max and his mother moved to be closer to his grandparents, and I went back to having my lunch with the rest of the staff. But for those few years, the “Summer Sandwich Club” brought joy to one camp counselor and many young campers.

皮克曼的模特
Pickman’s Model

不，我不知道皮克曼变成什么样了，也不想猜他的结局。你可能会认为当初我和他绝交的时候有什么难言之隐——是的，这就是我不想知道他现在身在何处的原因。把这个问题留给警察吧。考虑到他们至今还不知道他化名为彼得斯在北角区租了一间房子，我想他们也弄不出什么名堂来。我不确定自己是否还能找到那间房子，不过我可不愿做这样的尝试，哪怕在大白天也不行！

是的，我知道他留着那间房子的原因，或者说我害怕知道这个原因。别急，我马上就会谈到它了。我想不等我说完为什么我没有告诉警察那间房子，你就会明白这其中的原因了。如果我说了，他们就会让我带路去找这间房子；但是，即便我认得路，也不会再回到那里去了。那间屋子里有鬼——现在我都不敢乘地铁或者下地窖了（你尽管为此嘲笑我吧）。

我想你应该知道，我和皮克曼绝交可不是出于和那几个挑剔的老女人同样愚蠢的原因，像里德博士、乔·迈诺特，或者罗斯沃思。病态的艺术风格可吓不倒我。如果一个人拥有像皮克曼那样的天赋，那么能够认识他对我来说是莫大的荣幸，我才不管他的作品是什么风格呢。理查德·厄普顿·皮克曼堪称波士顿有史以来最伟大的画家。我第一次看到他的作品的时候，就做了如此评价，现在依然这么认为。即便他展出了那幅《食尸鬼的盛宴》，我依然丝毫不改初衷。你应该还记得，那幅画就是迈诺特和他绝交的原因。

你知道，要创作出像皮克曼那样水平的作品，需要深厚的艺术造诣和对大自然的深刻的洞察力。随便哪位二流的杂志封面画家胡乱画上一通，都可以称之为噩梦，女巫的安息日，或者魔鬼的肖像。但是只有伟大的画家才可能创造出如此栩栩如生的东西，让人看一眼就不寒而栗。只有一位真正的艺术家才明白真正的解剖恐怖感或者生理层面的害怕，达到一种只有具有潜在本能或遗传惊恐记忆的人才能达到的程度，也只有真正的艺术家笔下的颜色对比和光线效果才能激起休眠的奇异感。富塞利的一幅作品可以让我们吓得浑身发抖，而那些廉价的鬼故事插画只会惹我们发笑。这其中的原因不需要我来告诉你了吧。那些家伙可以看到一些超生命的东西；借助他们的作品，我们也可以一窥超越我们感知力的未知世界。关于这一点，多雷做到了，赛姆做到了，芝加哥的安加罗拉也做到了。而皮克曼达到的水平真可谓前无古人——老天，希望也后无来者。

千万别问我他们究竟看到了什么。你知道的，对一般的艺术家而言，作画对象是生机勃勃的大自然或活生生的模特，要比循规蹈矩地窝在简陋的画室里对着一辆人造的小卡车作画好得多，两者的作画效果会有天壤之别。但是，对于一位真正的天才就要另当别论了：天才艺术家有一种独特的视野，能将自已看到的光怪陆离的虚幻世界作为自己作画的模特或者真实场景。总之，正如画家会尽力让自已的作品有别于函授学校漫画家的大杂烩一样，这些天才也会设法创造出有别于冒牌艺术家的甜美馅饼梦一样的作品。如果我能看见皮克曼所看到的东西——不，还是看不见的好。我的老天爷，如果我真的看到了那个男人——如果他还可以称之为人的话——所看到的东西，我现在一定不在人世了。现在，让我们先喝杯酒，然后跟你细谈。

你还记得吧，皮克曼最擅长的是画人物肖像。在西班牙绘画大师戈雅之后，我认为没有人可以将那么多纯地狱般的情景表现在一组人物身上，或扭曲的表情上。戈雅之前，只有中世纪的雕刻艺术家在给巴黎圣母院和圣米歇尔山雕刻鬼怪雕像的时候做到了这一点。他们相信他们所雕刻的东西，或许还亲眼看到过，因为中世纪的时候，人们还是比较迷信鬼怪的。我记得在你离开那年，你自己也曾问过皮克曼，他到底从哪里得到了这些怪异的构思和幻象。他对你的问题报之一笑，那笑容够诡异邪恶吧？里德之所以与他绝交，部分原因就是那笑容。你知道当时里德刚刚开始学习比较病理学，脑袋里充满了各种浮夸理论，认为精神或者生理疾病产生的原因是生物遗传或进化的结果。他说他一天比一天更加厌恶皮克曼，最后简直有点儿害怕见到他——那个家伙的外貌和表情在慢慢变化，变得让他越来越不喜欢，越来越不像人类。他还经常讨论饮食，并且断言皮克曼肯定古怪异常到了极点。如果你和里德保持着联系的话，我猜你告诉过他，说皮克曼的画让他神经紧张或者饱受折磨。其实我也告诉过他。

Pickman' s Model

No, I don't know what's become of Pickman, and I don't like to guess. You might have surmised I had some inside information when I dropped him—and that's why I don't want to think where he's gone. Let the police find what they can—it won't be much, judging from the fact that they don't know yet of the old North End place he hired under the name of Peters. I'm not sure that I could find it again myself—not that I'd ever try, even in broad daylight!

Yes, I do know, or I am afraid I know, why he maintained it. I'm coming to that. And I think you'll understand before I'm through why I don't tell the police. They would ask me to guide them, but I couldn't go back there even if I knew the way. There was something there–and now I can't use the subway or (and you may as well have your laugh at this, too) go down into cellars any more.

I should think you'd have known I didn't drop Pickman for the same silly reasons that Dr. Reid or Joe Minot or Rosworth did. Morbid art doesn't shock me, and when a man has the genius Pickman had I feel it an honour to know him, no matter what direction his work takes. Boston never had a greater painter than Richard Upton Pickman. I said it at first and I say it still, and I never swerved an inch, either, when he showed that

"Ghoul Feeding". That, you remember, was when Minot cut him.

You know, it takes profound art and profound insight into Nature to turn out stuff like Pickman's. Any magazine-cover hack can splash paint around wildly and call it a nightmare or a Witches' Sabbath or a portrait of the devil, but only a great painter can make such a thing really scare or ring true. That's because only a real artist knows the actual anatomy of the terrible or the physiology of fear—the exact sort of lines and proportions that connect up with latent instincts or hereditary memories of fright, and the proper color contrasts and lighting effects to stir the dormant sense of strangeness. I don't have to tell you why a Fuseli really brings a shiver while a cheap ghost-story frontispiece merely makes us laugh. There's something those fellows catch—beyond life—that they're able to make us catch for a second. Doré had it. Sime has it. Angarola of Chicago has it. And Pickman had it as no man ever had it before or—I hope to Heaven—ever will again.

Don't ask me what it is they see. You know, in ordinary art, there's all the difference in the world between the vital, breathing things drawn from Nature or models and the artificial truck that commercial small fry reel off in a bare studio by rule. Well, I should say that the really weird artist has a kind of vision which makes models, or summons up what amounts to actual scenes from the spectral world he lives in. Anyhow, he manages to turn out results that differ from the pretender's mince-pie dreams in just about the same way that the life painter's results differ from the concoctions of a correspondence-school cartoonist. If I had ever seen what Pickman saw—

but no! Here, let's have a drink before we get any deeper. God, I wouldn't be alive if I'd ever seen what that man—if he was a man—saw!

You recall that Pickman's forte was faces. I don't believe anybody since Goya could put so much of sheer hell into a set of features or a twist of expression. And before Goya you have to go back to the mediaeval chaps who did the gargoyles and chimaeras on Notre Dame and Mont Saint-Michel. They believed all sorts of things—and maybe they saw all sorts of things, too, for the Middle Ages had some curious phases. I remember your asking Pickman yourself once, the year before you went away, wherever in thunder he got such ideas and visions. Wasn't that a nasty laugh he gave you? It was partly because of that laugh that Reid dropped him. Reid, you know, had just taken up comparative pathology, and was full of pompous "inside stuff" about the biological or evolutionary significance of this or that mental or physical symptom. He said Pickman repelled him more and more every day, and almost frightened him towards the last—that the fellow's features and expression were slowly developing in a way he didn't like; in a way that wasn't human. He had a lot of talk about diet, and said Pickman must be abnormal and eccentric to the last degree. I suppose you told Reid, if you and he had any correspondence over it, that he'd let Pickman's paintings get on his nerves or harrow up his imagination. I know I told him that myself—then.

友谊 Friendship

卡罗琳·叶和玛塞拉·安之间的故事说来话长。在她们二十多岁的时候，两个人都住在马萨诸塞州的剑桥镇；在过去的几年里，她们曾是最好的朋友——真可谓形影不离。后来，她们在同一时间发表了各自的第一本书：玛塞拉的书是由纽约一家大型的出版社出版的，而卡罗琳的书则是由一家虽然小有名气但规模很小的出版社出版的。她们俩的封面照非常相似：两个人看起来都神情肃穆，气质高贵，一身盛装，长发飘飘。这真是一个不幸的巧合，这让评论家不得不对她们进行一番对比，他们甚至揶揄地称她们为“东方长发诗人”“东方大辫儿”和“新晋的亚裔长发女诗人”。

但是这些嘲讽对玛塞拉产生的影响相对比较小。她的书受到重视，而她本人甚至被比作玛丽安·摩尔以及艾米丽·狄金森。她的诗内容丰富，开篇通常是对鸟类或者植物的一般看法，而后笔锋一转，将思绪转向一些抽象的主题，如混沌和惯性、圣经、进化、死亡等，其间还穿插少许对缺乏个性的看法。至少评论家是这么说的。迪安从图书馆借来了这本书，却搞不懂它在讲些什么。

与此相反，卡罗琳的书受到了各种指责。她的写作风格比较大众化，惯用俚语，内容多是热门话题和流行文化。她在书中还谈到了玛丽莲·梦露和蘑菇鸡片、外星婴儿，以及她本人对家禽奇怪的、傻乎乎的痴迷。评论家对她草草地做了评价：平庸的人才。

卡罗琳说，接下来发生的事情更糟糕。玛塞拉在各个方面都让她感到一种深深的挫败感。教学工作的机会，在杂志上发表文章，奖品或肯定——卡罗琳努力申请的每样东西，玛塞拉都轻而易举地得到了。这些本没有什么不对，玛塞拉脸皮很厚，又能说会道，可以跟任何一个对她可能有用的人肆无忌惮地调情，并迅速建立工作关系，背后又会对别人大肆嘲讽。问题的关键是，玛塞拉非常富有。她的父亲是位船业大亨。她本人拥有数百万元的信托资金。所以，那些可怜的挂名职务对她而言，根本不算什么，但是对卡罗琳而言，那些却是她赖以生存的谋生之道。显而易见，玛塞拉之所以争取这些，就是为了看她的笑话。

“她真是一只秃鹰，一个吸血鬼，”卡罗琳告诉迪安，“你知道的吧，她从来不在白天的时候出门，她经常熬夜到凌晨四五点钟才睡觉，一直睡到午后才起床。”

然后她又谈到了伊万的事。伊万是一家文学杂志社的英语—意大利语编辑，曾经和卡罗琳谈了七年恋爱，耐心地等待着他们能步入婚姻的殿堂，能够生儿育女。但是，他突然在某天跟卡罗琳提出分手，并且没有给出任何理由。卡罗琳追问他提出分手的原因，说如果不给出一个答案，就不肯放他走。他最终作了让步。“因为玛塞拉告诉了我一些事情。”他承认道。

起初，卡罗琳还担心是他们之间有了私情，后来却发现真实情况比她想象的邪恶得多。“玛塞拉告诉我说她很崇拜我，”伊万说，“她说她永远也不会像我这么慷慨大方。她还说如果一个男人的工作不能赢得她的尊敬，她是不可能和他在一起的。我认真考虑了她所说的话，觉得自己根本不像她说的那样慷慨。她的话侵蚀着我的内心，让我寝食难安。我忍受不了这些话。”

卡罗琳逃到了加利福尼亚州，最后定居在罗萨里托湾一个名不见经传的小镇上。她决定让自己完全脱离诗歌的世界。她依然坚持每天写点儿什么，毕竟这是她的爱好，虽然很折磨人，但是六年来，她从未去尝试发表任何东西。她已经三十七岁了，现在是一位服务员——上午在一家小餐馆负责早餐，下午在一家烧烤店负责晚餐。因为长时间站立的关系，她的脚大了一码。她现在一文不名，但是觉得渐渐找回了原来的自己，并且更健康，更放松，也睡得更香了。她说她能有今天，迪安功不可没。她过得很开心——或者说像一位诗人一样开心。

Friendship

Caroline Yip and Marcella Ahn had a history. They had both lived in Cambridge, Massachusetts, in their twenties, and for several years, they had been the best of friends—inseparable, really. But then their first books had come out at the same time, Marcella's from a major New York publisher, Caroline's from a small, albeit respected press. Both had very similar jacket photos, the two women looking solemn and precious, hair flowing in full regalia. An unfortunate coincidence. Critics couldn't resist reviewing them together, mocking the pair, even then, as "The Hair Poets," "The Braids of the East," and "The New Asian Poe-tresses."

But Marcella escaped these barbs relatively unscathed. Her book was taken seriously, and she was even compared to Marianne Moore and Emily Dickinson. Her poetry was highly erudite, usually beginning with mundane observations about birds or plant life, then slipping into long, abstract meditations on entropy and inertia, the Bible, evolution, and death, punctuated by the briefest mention of personal deprivations. Or so the critics said. Dean still had the book from the library, and he couldn't make heads or tails of it.

In contrast, Caroline's book had been skewered. She wrote in a slangy, contemporary voice, full of topical, popculture allusions. She wrote about

Marilyn Monroe and moo goo gai pan, about alien babies and her strange, loopy obsession with poultry. She was roundly dispatched as a mediocre talent.

Worse, Caroline said, was what happened afterwards. Marcella began to thwart her at every turn. Teaching jobs, coveted magazine publications, awards—everything Caroline applied for, Marcella got. It didn't hurt that Marcella was a shameless schmoozer, flirting and networking with anyone who might be of use, all the while ridiculing them behind their backs. The fact was, Marcella was rich. Her father was a shipping tycoon, and she had a trust fund in the millions. She didn't need any of these pitifully small sinecures which would have meant a livelihood to Caroline, and it became obvious that the only reason Marcella was pursuing them at all was to taunt her.

"She's a vulture, a vampire," Caroline told Dean. "You know she won't go out in the light of day? She stays up until four, five in the morning and doesn't wake up until past noon."

And then there was the matter of Evan Paviromo, the English-Italian editor of a literary journal whom Caroline had dated for seven years, waiting patiently for them to get married and have children. He broke it off one day without explanation. She dogged him. Why? Why was he ending it? She refused to let him go without some sort of answer. Finally he complied. "It's something Marcella said," he admitted.

At first Caroline feared they were involved romantically, but the truth was more vicious. "Marcella told me she admired me," Evan said, "that I was far more generous than she could ever be. She said she just wouldn't be able to stay with someone whose work she didn't really respect. I thought about that, and I decided I'm not that generous after all. It's something that would eat away at me, that's bothered me all along. It's something I can't abide."

Caroline fled to California, eventually landing in the little nondescript town of Rosarita Bay. She completely disengaged herself from the poetry world. She was still writing every day, excruciating as it was for her, but she had not attempted to publish anything in six years. She was thirty-seven now, and a waitress—the breakfast shift at a diner, the dinner shift at a barbecue joint. Her feet had grown a full size from standing so much, and she was broke. But she had started to feel like her old self again, healthier, more relaxed, sleeping better. Dean had a lot to do with it, she said. She was happy—or as happy as it was possible for a poet to be.

这山望着那山高
The Grass is Always Greener

我曾经非常向往加利福尼亚州温暖的气候和灿烂的阳光，但自从从纽约的布法罗搬到南加州后，我发现自己比想象中更怀念以前的天气。身处一个一年四季都阳光明媚的地方，我开始特别向往四季分明的气候。

当我居住在布法罗的时候，我过得很不开心，因为我热爱冲浪，但是布法罗根本没有地方让我冲浪。我梦想住在海边，一年到头都可以晒太阳，还能享受美味的墨西哥食物——所有这些在布法罗是不可能实现的。所以我特别想搬到加州去。

最后，我在加州找到一份工作，并搬去了加州的奥兰治县。但当我到那里以后，我发现事情和我想象中的完全不一样。我惊讶地发现自己竟然开始怀念四季的变化。在经历了连续四个月的好天气以后，我最想看到的就是树叶的颜色发生一点儿变化。

我去了海边，但是并没有去冲浪。我坐在沙滩上埋头写日志，倾诉自己对纽约的无比思念之情。我思念着那里的秋季：采摘苹果，开车去郊外欣赏落叶，享受万圣节夜晚那种清冽寒冷的天气。没有传统活动的圣诞节让人找不到一点儿节日的感觉，以前圣诞节期间我们会装饰圣诞树，堆雪人，玩了一天的雪橇以后会围在火堆前取暖，等等。春天到来的时候，也没有一如既往地给人带来如释重负和生机勃勃的感觉；因为在加州，春天好像是绵绵无尽头的，所以春天的开始没有给人带来什么不同的感觉。

我一直认为“这山望着那山高”这句格言是无稽之谈，但是在我搬到加州之后，我开始体会到这句话蕴含的意义。当我住在布法罗的时候，我希望能够搬到加州去；当我真的搬到了加州，我又开始怀念在布法罗的生活。我似乎没办法让自己过得很开心。

最后，我终于找到一个可以让自己开心的办法：我搬去了科德角。在那里，我既可以在夏天冲浪，又能够尽情享受四季分明的变化。

The Grass is Always Greener

I used to long for the warmth and sun of California, but after moving to Southern California from Buffalo, New York, I missed the seasons more than I ever thought I would. In a place where it's sunny all the time, I longed for winter, spring, summer, and fall.

When I lived in Buffalo, I was unhappy because I love to surf, and of course I couldn't do it in Buffalo. I dreamed of beaches, a year–round tan, and good Mexican food–all things I couldn't get in Buffalo. I wanted to move to California so badly.

Finally, I got a job and moved to Orange County. When I got there, it wasn't what I'd expected at all. To my surprise, I missed the seasons. After about four months of perfect weather, all I wanted was to see the leaves change color.

When I went to the beach, I didn't go surfing, I sat on the sand and wrote in my journal about how much I missed New York. I missed the fall: picking apples, going for long drives to look at the foliage, and enjoying crisp, cold Halloween nights. It didn't feel like Christmas without the traditions like decorating the tree, building snowmen, and sitting by a real fire after a day of sledding. And when spring came it didn't bring with it the usual feelings of relief and renewal. It had felt like spring for months and months, so the technical beginning of spring didn't make any difference.

I'd always thought the aphorism "the grass is always greener on the other side of the fence" was a stupid one. However, once I'd moved to California, that saying suddenly made sense. When I was in Buffalo, I wanted to be in California, and when I was in California, I wanted to be in Buffalo. I couldn't seem to please myself.

Eventually, I found a solution that makes me very happy. I moved to Cape Cod, where I can surf in the summer and still enjoy the changing of the seasons and luxuriate in the ever-volatile temperament of the weather.

【第二章】
NO.2

精英人物

The Elites

世界语文·美国语文
International Literature American Literature
2

李·福尔克和他的漫画

Lee Falk and His Cartoon Comics

李·福尔克于1999年去世，他生前完成了两部成功的漫画作品：《魔术师曼德拉克》和《轰天奇兵》。这两部作品分别于1935年和1937年首次出版，是当时由原作者独立完成的最早的漫画作品。一些漫画作品年代更早，但由于原作者去世或者退休，都不是由原作者独立完成的。

福尔克的首部成功作品是《魔术师曼德拉克》。它讲述的是一位魔术师和逃亡艺术家的故事，就像20世纪早期的大魔术师胡迪尼一样，在世界各地经历各种各样的冒险。该部作品现在依然被很多报纸刊载。

福尔克另外一部更加成功的作品是《轰天奇兵》。漫画的主角巴哈姆特身着紫色紧身衣，头戴黑色面具，骑着一匹白马，所到之处都有他忠实的狼狗相陪。他住在一个森林王国，坐在一个骷髅头形的宝座上统治着他的王国。福尔克创造的这位紫衣英雄不仅仅出现在报纸上，还成了周六上午专为儿童播放的动画片和电视连续剧里的大明星。在20世纪90年代，这部作品还被拍摄成了完整版的电影。但是由于没有使用昂贵的特效和追车场面，这部影片没有引起太大轰动。

第二次世界大战期间，巴哈姆特和一切与民主为敌的人展开了恶斗，比如法西斯主义者。为此，意大利的独裁者墨索里尼和西班牙的独裁者佛朗哥将该漫画列为禁书。在德国占领挪威期间，巴哈姆特在斯堪的纳维亚半岛尤其受欢迎，成了顽强抵抗侵略者的象征。现在，巴哈姆特的受欢迎程度一点儿也没有下降。瑞典还修建了一座巴哈姆特主题公园。

和布鲁斯·韦恩及克拉克·肯特（蝙蝠侠和超人的另一种身份）一样，巴哈姆特也有双重身份。但和后来创造出来的超人、蝙蝠侠、蜘蛛侠等超级英雄形象不同的是，巴哈姆特没有超能力。他不能透过建筑物看东西，也没有飞檐走壁的本领。但六十多年来，他一直用自己的力量击败犯罪分子，赶走邪恶力量，而自己从来不伤一分一毫。并且，身穿紫衣的他，看起来依然很强壮。

Lee Falk and His Cartoon Comics

Lee Falk, who died in 1999, was the author of two successful comic strips, *Mandrake the Magician* and *The Phantom*. First published in 1935 and 1937 respectively, they were the oldest comic strips written continuously by the original author. Some strips are older, but they are no longer written by their first author, who has died or retired.

Falk's first success was *Mandrake the Magician*. It is the story of a magician and escape artist, like the great Houdini of early in the twentieth century, who has adventures all over the world. It is still carried by many newspapers.

An even greater hit was *The Phantom*. The Phantom wears a sort of purple body-stocking and a black mask. He rides white horse and is accompanied by his faithful wolf-dog. The Phantom lives in a jungle kingdom which he rules from a skull-shaped throne. Appearing not only in newspapers, Falk's purple-clad hero became a star in cartoons and serials shown for kids on Saturday mornings. *The Phantom* became a full-length movie in the 1990s, but because it didn't have expensive special effects and car chases, it was not a big hit.

Like Bruce Wayne or Clark kent, the alter-egos of Batman and Superman, the Phantom also has a dual identity. During the Second World

War, the Phantom fought against the enemies of democracy, like the Fascists. The dictators Mussolini, in Italy, and Franco, in Spain, banned the comic. Especially popular in Scandinavia, the Phantom was a symbol of the Resistance during the German occupation of Norway. The popularity of the figure has not declined. In Sweden, there is a Phantom theme park today.

Like Brule Wayne or Clark Kent, the alter−egos of Batman and Superman, the phantom also has a dual identity. Unlike the superheroes like Superman, Batman, or Spiderman, who came later, the Phantom does not have supernatural power. He cannot see through buildings, or fly, or stick to the ceiling. He still has managed to fight crime and stomp out evil for over sixty years without getting himself killed. And he still looks fit in his purple suit.

给海伦·凯勒带来光明的人

Helen Keller’s Light in the Darkness

海伦·凯勒生于1880年。她像其他健全的孩子一样开始自己的人生，她快乐、健康，和同龄人一样牙牙学语，蹒跚学步。她在两岁生日前被一场高烧夺去视力和听力，从此开始了不平凡的人生旅程。虽然引起海伦高烧的原因当时从未得到确诊，但是现代的医生认为海伦得的是脑膜炎。这场疾病把海伦推入了无声的黑暗深渊，那种感受是大多数人无法想象的。凯勒夫妇的第一个孩子竟然成了聋盲人。

开始几年的生活对海伦来说充满了沮丧，她的家人也是身心俱疲。海伦经常在自己家里徘徊摸索，急于体验一些新感觉，却理解不了所碰到的任何东西。这让她变得很愤怒。随着年龄的增长，她的脾气也越来越暴躁。海伦的父母为她遭受的不幸感到难过，所以对她的坏脾气持无限包容的态度。眼看海伦的脾气越来越难以控制，为了避免女儿被送往州精神病院，凯勒夫妇作了最后的努力。他们联系了马萨诸塞州波士顿市的帕金斯研究所。这家研究所主要是为盲童开设的，不过它的教工曾帮助过一个又盲又聋的孩子。

研究所派来了安妮·沙利文老师。她真可谓海伦生命中的奇迹创造者。沙利文老师认为海伦只有通过自我约束才能战胜她面临的巨大挑战。但是海伦父母对女儿一贯的溺爱常常使安妮的努力发挥不了应有的作用。

海伦的顽固任性真是让人精疲力竭。但安妮明白，如果给予正确的引导，海伦的顽固会成为她自己的救星。为了创造奇迹，安妮需要让海伦远离父母的骄纵。在得到海伦父母的允许后，她带着海伦到凯勒夫妇花园对面的小屋生活。刚开始，海伦依然不配合安妮的工作，但是在安妮的坚持下，海伦慢慢变得听话顺从。很快，海伦的这种顺从变成了对安妮的信任。海伦渐渐开始明白她所碰触到的每一个东西都是有名字的。这一新发现给她的黑暗世界带来一丝光明，也唤醒了她永无止境的求知欲。

在以后的日子里，安妮·沙利文继续不断满足海伦对学习的渴求，给她无边的黑暗世界带来了一束不灭的光。

Helen Keller's Light in the Darkness

Helen Keller was born in 1880. Her life began normally. She was happy and healthy, learning to walk and talk like her toddler peers. It was not until a high fever robbed her of sight and hearing just before her second birthday that her life began its remarkable journey. Although the exact cause of Helen's fever was never determined, modern doctors believed Helen suffered from meningitis. The illness plunged Helen into a dark silence that most people cannot even imagine. The Kellers' beloved first-born child was blind and deaf.

The next few years were frustrating for Helen and physically and emotionally draining for her family. Helen wandered around the family's property, anxious to discover new sensations but unable to understand anything that she experienced. Her resulting tantrums became more violent as she continued to grow. Feeling sorry for their impaired daughter, Helen's parents allowed the tantrums to occur with no consequences. In a last-ditch effort to keep the increasingly unmanageable Helen from being sent to the State Insane Asylum, the Kellers contacted the Perkins Institute in Boston, Massachusetts. Primarily just a school for the blind, its staff had once helped a child who was both blind and deaf.

Enter Annie Sullivan, who truly became the "miracle worker" in

Helen's life. Only with self-discipline would Helen be able to overcome her tremendous challenges. Unfortunately, Helen's parents' constant coddling of their daughter was undermining Annie's efforts.

Helen's stubbornness was exhausting, but Annie knew that, if channeled, it would be Helen's salvation. In order to work her "miracle," Annie needed to get Helen away from her parents' pampering. Annie was given permission to take Helen to live in a little house on the opposite side of the Kellers' garden. Initially, Helen continued to fight Annie's efforts, but gradually the girl began to behave. Soon, Helen's submission became trust in Annie. Helen began to comprehend that everything she touched had a name. Her constant darkness was suddenly illuminated by this new-found understanding, and her hunger for knowledge became insatiable.

For the remainder of her life, Annie Sullivan continued to feed Helen's appetite for learning, providing a constant light in Helen's otherwise impenetrable darkness.

特哈诺音乐及其第一人

Tejano Music and Its Meadowlark

特哈诺是20世纪发展起来的最为活跃的一种民族音乐形式。特哈诺音乐也被称为得克萨斯——墨西哥音乐或边境音乐，因为特哈诺起源于得克萨斯州和墨西哥交界的地方。这种音乐形式融合了西班牙、德国和英格兰等地的传统音乐风格。

19世纪末期，部分德国人移居到美国得克萨斯州南部和墨西哥北部地区。他们随身携带了自己钟爱的纽扣手风琴，当然还有他们擅长的舞蹈音乐，比如波尔卡和华尔兹。当地音乐家不仅采用了他们带来的乐器，还接受了他们的音乐形式。他们也开始在自己的舞蹈音乐中弹奏手风琴。同时，西班牙和英格兰民谣也以叙事的形式植根于特哈诺音乐之中，以这种音乐形式讲述这些地区城镇及牧场里发生的有关勇敢、浪漫和悲惨的故事。最终，在二重奏的歌唱和包括手风琴、鼓、立式贝司、五弦琴和西班牙十二弦低音吉他在内的乐器组合的基础上，一种独特的音乐风格就这样诞生了。这种音乐风格被称为康芬特音乐。康芬特音乐成了特哈诺音乐的核心。

第一位因演唱特哈诺音乐而出名的音乐家是莉迪亚·门多萨，她于1916年出生于墨西哥，但后来她随全家移居到了美国。门多萨全家以在农场做工和巡回演唱为生。莉迪亚从各种各样的泡泡糖包装纸上学到了很多歌曲里的生词。当时很多音乐发行商喜欢将歌词印刷在泡泡糖纸上，希望通过这种方式扩大自己的知名度。

1928年，莉迪亚和她的家人在得克萨斯州南部圣安东尼奥市录制了第一张唱片。她清澈且生动的演唱风格迅速使其脱颖而出，成为美国北部和南部以西班牙语为主的地方的一名新秀。

接下来一些音乐家继承了莉迪亚的演唱风格，扩大了特哈诺音乐的影响。像其他民族音乐一样，特哈诺音乐以其紧凑的旋律、丰富的内涵和多变的韵律赢得大家的喜爱，且保持经久不衰的活力。

Tejano Music and Its Meadowlark

One of the liveliest folk music forms to develop in the twentieth century is Tejano music. Also known as Tex-Mex or border music because of its origins on both side of the Texas-Mexico border, this form combine elements from Spanish, German and English musical traditions.

In the late nineteenth century, German immigrants to south Texas and northern Mexico brought with them their dance music Polkas and Waltzes and the button accordion. The music and the instrument were adopted by musicians in that region, who began to use the accordion in their own dance music, huapangos and rancheras. At the same time, the Spanish and English folk ballad traditions took root in Tejano music in form of corridos, narrative songs of bravery, romance, and tragedy set in the towns and ranches of the region. Eventually, a unique musical style developed based on duet singing and an instrumentation of accordion, drums, upright bass, and bajo sexto, the Spanish twelve-string bass guitar. This style, known as conjunto, it became the heart of Tejano music.

The first Tejano musician to gain status was Lydia Mendoza. She was born in Mexico in 1916, but her family soon immigrated to the United States. The Mendoza family made their living on working alternately as field hands and as touring musicians. Mendoza learned the words to many of her songs from bubble gum wrappers, where music publishers had song lyrics printedin the hope of making them popular.

In 1928 in San Antonio, Texas, Mendoza and her family made their first recording. Her clear and expressive singing style soon gained her widespread popularity in the Spanish-speaking regions of North and South America.

Others have followed Lydia Mendoza's lead and have expanded the influence of Tejano music. Like other folk music forms, Tejano music has an intensity, literary richness, and rhythmic variety that ensures its continued vitality.

J.R.R.托尔金和我
J.R.R. Tolkien and Me

约翰·罗纳德·瑞尔·托尔金，一般简称为J.R.R.托尔金。托尔金的一生有很多头衔，包括语言学者、作家和大学教授。当然，现在大多数人记得他，是因为他完成了小说巨著《魔戒三部曲》，这部小说后来被拍成了一部史诗电影。

在我十岁的时候，我的朋友艾琳向我推荐了托尔金的作品。艾琳给了我一本《霍比特人》，并且告诉我说每天吃过晚饭后她的父亲会在餐桌旁读《魔戒》给她和她的弟弟听。一打开《霍比特人》，我就被这部作品深深吸引住了。在我十四岁的时候，我已经读完了托尔金所有的魔幻小说。

随着阅读的深入，我不但对托尔金创造的魔幻世界越来越着迷，对他本人也产生了浓厚的兴趣。我开始梦想有一天能见到托尔金本人。我想象着有一天到他执教的牛津大学参观，亲自登门拜访这位英语语言和文学教授，告诉他他的作品对我来说意义是多么重大。

但是，对于生活在美国中西部的我来说，去英国参观旅行的可能性似乎很小。后来我知道托尔金在我开始读《霍比特人》之前已经去世很多年了。于是，我就把这个梦想放在一边，全身心地投入学习、运动和申请大学等诸多事情上。

我在大学主修的专业是化学，但是在大学二年级的时候，我选的专业课程不太多。大三的时候，我参加了学校的荣誉英语项目，这让我有机会接触到学校的中世纪和文艺复兴研究委员会。委员会的主任认为我非常适合申请他新开发的一个文凭项目——介于本科生和研究生之间的过渡项目。我提出并通过了申请，结果发现我有机会实现从前的梦想了：我要前往英国，去牛津大学，那可是我最喜爱的作家的故乡。

牛津大学和美国的很多大学都不一样。它不是一个统一的整体，而是由三十九个独立学院组成的联合体。每所学院都有自己独立的内部组织结构和活动设置，在组织考试和授予学位方面又彼此交叉管理。例如，托尔金曾是默顿学院的一位教授，他的好友C.S.路易斯在莫德林学院执教。大部分的学生会认为自己属于某所学院，而不是这所大学。这就意味着穿着印有牛津大学字样运动衫的人一般都是游客。

我爱牛津的一切。我爱那些幽深的小巷：巷子两边的店面都在茂密树冠的庇荫之下，远远看去，只能看到附近公园里连绵的山丘和坐落其中的高高的中世纪塔楼。我爱牛津鲜活的历史感：孩子们在教堂后院的参天大树下玩耍，无忧无虑地穿梭在教堂后院的那些有几百年历史的墓碑丛中；或者听我们的管家向我们讲述阿拉伯的劳伦斯的幽灵据说就住在我们的小区的故事。当一股股莫名其妙的气流从我的房间飘过的时候，我们的管家说那一定是劳伦斯的幽灵。我喜欢每周二走路去上我的民俗学课。沿途会路过一家叫雄鹰和孩子的小酒吧，当年，托尔金就是在这儿和他的好朋友一起讨论创作思路的。据说《霍比特人》里的比尔博骑着巨鹰飞行的构思就是受到了酒吧标志的启发。最棒的一点是，我的一位任课教授认识托尔金本人。

本尼迪克塔修女是一位非常聪明而又和善的修女。虽然上了点年纪，但是在她身上却看不到那种死气沉沉的学究气。在她刚受聘于圣史蒂芬学院的时候，作为托尔金的同事，她曾与他有过一段时间的接触。有一天，她问我在牛津学习的感觉怎么样，我决定告诉她我的梦想。我告诉她当我还是个孩子的时候，我就非常渴望见到托尔金。我大脑里曾浮现过这样一幅生动的画面：我来到牛津，找到了他的小屋，穿过栅栏和玫瑰丛，最终敲响了这个伟大男人的家门。我甚至想象过他打开门，然后看着我。只是我不曾想好要说什么，才能让自己看起来不像个彻头彻尾的傻瓜。

本尼迪克塔修女放声大笑起来，然后对我说："他会鼓励你这种感觉的。"显然，很多人觉得托尔金是一位祖父般的绅士，但是，除非你是他的孙子，他才会这样。他经常很严肃，并不十分友好。我想他之所以这样，是为了让自己成为一位更好的教授。我很高兴最终实现了我的牛津之旅，但遗憾的是，我永远也没有机会向托尔金本人当面道谢。

J.R.R. Tolkien and Me

John Ronald Reuel Tolkien, better known as J.R.R. Tolkien, was many things in his long life, including philologist, writer, and university professor. Of course, today, most people remember him as the author of The *Lord of the Rings*— a monumental work that became an epic film.

A friend introduced me to Tolkien's writings when I was 10 years old. Aileen gave me a copy of *The Hobbit*, and told me her father was reading *The Lord of the Rings* to her and her brother at the dinner table every night after the family had finished eating. I read The Hobbit and was hooked. By the time I was 14, I had read every piece of fiction Tolkien had published.

The more I read, the more fascinated I became with not only the world Tolkien had created, but with the man himself. I began to dream of meeting Tolkien. I imagined someday traveling to Oxford University, where he had been a professor of English Language and Literature, and somehow finding the words to tell him how meaningful his writings had been for me.

But, growing up in the Midwest, the possibility of traveling to England seemed very remote. Then I discovered that Tolkien had died years before I'd even started reading The Hobbit. I forgot about my dream and got down to the business of school and sports and college applications.

I started college as a chemistry major, but by my sophomore year, I was major—less. Somehow, by my junior year, I was accepted into the Honors English program. This introduced me to the Medieval and Renaissance Collegium(MARC). The director of MARC thought I would be a perfect fit for a new diploma program he was developing—an interim program between undergraduate and graduate work. I applied, was accepted, and found myself faced with my old dream: I was headed to England—to Oxford University, the home of my favorite author!

Oxford isn't set up like most American universities. It's not a single uniform entity. Instead, it's a collection of 39 independent colleges, each with its own internal structure and activities, with an overlying administration that conducts examinations and confers degrees. Tolkien, for example, had been a professor at Merton College. His close friend, C.S.Lewis, taught at Magdalen College (pronounced: Mawdlin). Most students identify with their college, not with the university. This means that pretty much anyone there wearing an Oxford University sweatshirt is a tourist.

I loved Oxford. I loved the tiny streets and the way the trees hid the modern shop fronts, showing only the medieval towers from the rolling hills of a nearby park. Even more, I loved the sense of living history—the way the children would play carelessly under towering trees among centuries—old tombstones in the back yards of churches, or the stories our housekeeper would tell of Lawrence of Arabia's ghost who, apparently, lived in our own quarters. When inexplicable drafts would sweep through my room, our housekeeper swore it was Lawrence. I loved walking every Tuesday on my way to my folklore tutorial, past the pub—The Eagle and the Child–where Tolkien met with his best friends to discuss their ideas for writing. The sign on the pub allegedly was the inspiration for Bilbo's flight with the Giant Eagles. Best of all, I had a professor who had actually known J.R.R. Tolkien himself.

Sr. Benedicta was a very smart but very kindly, elderly nun. She was no slouch as an academic and had published several highly regarded books in her field. As a colleague, she had spent time with Tolkien when she was newly hired at St. Stephen's College. One day, when she had asked me how I liked studying at Oxford, I decided to tell her about my dream. I told her how, when I was a child, I had wanted so badly to meet Tolkien. I had vividly imagined traveling to Oxford, finding his little cottage, passing through the picket fence, past the rose bushes, to finally knock at the great man's door. I had even imagined him opening it and looking at me. I just could never, ever, think of anything to say that didn't make me feel like a complete idiot.

Sr. Benedicta smiled indulgently at me for a moment, and then said, "He would have encouraged that feeling." Apparently, most people have this impression of Tolkien as a gentle, grandfatherly sort of man, but, unless you were his grandchild, that wasn't actually the case. In person, he was frequently severe and not terribly friendly. I suppose it probably made him a better professor. In the end, I was very glad I finally made my pilgrimage to Oxford, but considered it for the best that I never had a chance to thank J.R.R. Tolkien in person.

玛丽·罗宾逊：我的演艺之路
The Memoirs of Mary Robinson

在我第一次登台演出那天，剧院里坐满了穿着入时的观众；演员休息室和管弦乐队边上挤满了评论家。我穿着一件绉纱滚边的浅粉色缎面礼服，到处点缀着闪闪发光的银色饰物。我的头上装饰着白色的羽毛；最后一幕中我穿的是一件极其简单的白色缎子衣服，好在我戴着用最透明的薄纱制成的长面纱，从头的后部一直垂到脚跟，腰间还缠绕着一串珍珠。

当我来到在舞台侧厅的时候，我的心开始狂跳不止；我开始担心我的决心会垮掉。我靠在保姆的胳膊上，几乎要晕过去了。谢里登先生和其他几位朋友鼓励我继续向前走。最终，我满怀担心和恐惧，四肢哆嗦地来到了观众面前。

观众席上响起的如雷般的掌声让我受宠若惊，几乎忘记了如何表演。我像个哑巴一样站在那里，慌乱地向观众鞠了一躬，过了好一会儿才虚弱无力地说出了第一场戏里的短短几句话。从始至终，我都不敢向观众席看一眼。

回到休息室后，我又一次受到大家的鼓励，至少我的外表看起来还是值得肯定的，但是我的个人能力却完全没有展示出来，因为我的恐惧影响了我的声音和表演。第二场戏是化装舞会，我有点儿时间让自己镇定下来。我永远都不会忘记我第一次看向观众席的感觉。我看到一排排黑压压的脑袋，所有人的目光都集中在我身上，从观众的目光中，我看到了敬畏和肯定。

待我重拾信心后，我发现观众的掌声更加响亮了。晚上的演出引来了无数的喝彩，我也获得了各种赞誉。我生平第一次感受到那种无法用语言描述的快乐。我听到其中一个最令人着迷的男人，也是那个时期最杰出的表演天才向我表达了赞美之词，中间还夹杂着些许羡慕。

我出演的第二个角色是《斯卡布罗之旅》里面的阿曼达。这部话剧改编自范布勒的《旧病复发》。原本以为这是一部新剧的观众认为自己被欺骗了，表现出非常不满的情绪。耶茨夫人因为忍受不了观众的嘘声，离开了舞台，留下我一个人面对气愤的观众，我完全被吓傻了。一个人木然地在那里站了好一会儿。谢里登夫人在侧厅向我示意，希望我留在舞台上。那个时候尚在人世的坎伯兰公爵坐在包厢里让我鼓起勇气，“他们嘘的不是你，是剧本本身。”公爵殿下说。于是我行了个屈膝礼。这个小小的动作好像震惊了全场，接下来我听到一阵阵雷鸣般的掌声，令我倍受鼓舞。

我扮演的第三个角色是《亚历山大大帝》里的斯塔蒂拉。德鲁里巷剧院的所有人之一莱西先生扮演男主角亚历山大大帝，罗克珊娜一角由梅尔莫斯太太扮演。我的表演再次得到了观众的肯定和赞赏。那天晚上，我穿的蓝白色的戏服是仿照波斯戏服的款式制作的。尽管在舞台上看起来有些奇异，我既没有穿裙箍，也没有涂粉，脚上还穿了一双装饰华丽的凉鞋，所有这些让我看起来既美艳动人，又别具一格。

虽然我经常受到极力的追捧和赞美，但我扮演过的角色里最受欢迎的还是奥菲丽亚、朱丽叶和罗莎琳德。帕尔米拉也是我出演过的最受欢迎的角色之一。我扮演的最后一个角色是克雷文夫人的喜剧《微型画》里的哈里·雷维尔爵士，而片尾曲《爱尔兰寡妇》就成了我演艺生涯中的绝唱。

The Memoirs of Mary Robinson

On the day of my first performance, the theatre was crowded with fashionable spectators; the green room and orchestra were thronged with critics. My dress was a pale pink satin, trimmed with crepe, and richly spangled with silver. My head was ornamented with white feathers and my glorious suit, for the last scene, was white satin and completely plain, except that I wore a veil of the most transparent gauze, which fell quite to my feet from the back of my head, and a string of beads round my waist.

When I approached the side wing my heart throbbed convulsively; I then began to fear that my resolution would fail, and I learned upon the Nurse's arm, almost fainting. Mr. Sheridan and several other friends encouraged me to proceed; and at length, with trembling limbs and fearful apprehension, I approached the audience.

The thundering applause that greeted me nearly overpowered all my faculties. I stood mute and bending with alarm, which did not subside till I had feebly articulated the few sentences of the first short scene, during the whole of which I had never once ventured to look at the audience.

On my return to green room, I was again encouraged, as far as my looks were deemed deserving of approval; for of my powers nothing yet could be known, my fears having as it were affected both my voice and action. The second scene being the masquerade, I had time to collect myself. I never shall forget the sensation which rushed through my bosom when I first looked towards the pit. I beheld a gradual ascent of heads. All eyes were fixed upon me, and the sensation they conveyed was awfully impressive.

As I acquired courage, I found the applause augment; and the night was concluded with peals of loud approbation. I was complimented on all sides. I then experienced, for the first time in my life, a pleasure that language could not explain. I heard one of the most fascinating men, and the most distinguished geniuses of the age, honor me with partial admiration.

The second character which I played was Amanda, in *A Trip to Scarborough*. The play was altered from Vanbrugh's *Relapse*; and the audience, supposing it was a new piece, on finding themselves deceived, expressed a considerable degree of disapproval. I was terrified beyond imagination when Mrs. Yates, no longer able to bear the hissing of the audience, quitted the scene, and left me alone to encounter the audience. I stood for some moments as though I had been petrified. Mr. Sheridan, from the side wing, desired me not to quit the boards. The late Duke of Cumberland from the stage box, bade me take courage: "It is not you, but the play, this hiss," said his Royal Highness. I curtsied and that curtsey seemed to electrify the whole house, for a thundering appeal of encouraging applause followed.

The third character I played was Statira, in *Alexander the Great*. Mr. Lacey, then one of the proprietors of Drury Lane Theatre, was the hero of the night, and the part of Roxana was performed by Mrs. Melmoth. Again, I was received with great warmth and approval. My dress was white and blue, made after the Persian costume; and though it was then singular on the stage, I wore neither a hoop nor power; my feet were bound by richly ornamented sandals, and the whole dress was picturesque and characteristic.

Though I was always received with the most flattering approval, the characters in which I was most popular were Ophelia, Juliet, and Rosalind. Palmira was also one of my most approved representations. The last character that I played was Sir Harry Revel, in Lady Craven's comedy of *The Miniature Picture*; and the epilogue song in *The Irish Widow* was my last farewell to the labor of my profession.

天才建筑师高迪
Gaudi, the Genius Architect

世界上大多数著名的教堂，都以其规模与美丽著称，但是圣家族教堂凭借自身独特且惊人的设计而鹤立鸡群。这座坐落在巴塞罗那的天主教教堂就像一座独特且华丽的城堡一样让人叹为观止。它用果篮雕刻作为装饰，中央大殿映照着森林里的树木，怪异的尖顶以及美丽的螺旋楼梯，这些标志性的设计让圣家族教堂就如埃菲尔铁塔或自由女神像那样出名。而且，圣家族教堂也是最能反映他的设计者、有“奇特的天才”之称的安东尼·高迪的特点的作品。

如今，人们纷纷拥向巴塞罗那去一睹高迪建筑的奇观，包括米拉之家、巴特罗公寓、奎尔宫、奎尔公园，当然，圣家族教堂也包括在内，都是大家的必去之处。但是，当高迪第一次公布自己的作品时，没有人预测到他能有现在的知名度。当时的评论家们认为他的作品是丑陋可怕的，甚至将其与怪物和地下城作比较。就在50年前，高迪还不是大家公认的天才建筑师。

1852年，安东尼·高迪出生在西班牙北部一个小镇上的工匠家庭。16岁时，他搬去巴塞罗那完成中学教育，并开始学习建筑学。即便在这样的少年时期，他也是一位很有争议性的人物：他批评当时标准化的建筑学教育，认为课程缺乏创造力，因而经常逃学。最后，他勉强拿到了学位。他的校主任颇有见地地评价高迪：“他要么是个天才，要么是个疯子。”

毕业之后，高迪继续留在巴塞罗那。这座城市正在飞速成长，富有的投资商也在寻找艺术家为其设计现代、时尚的建筑。在二十几岁时，高迪遇到了他的终生资助人欧塞比·奎尔——一位富有的实业家、政治家。在接下来近40年的时间里，奎尔资助高迪完成了大量作品：从奎尔的私人宅邸（奎尔宫），到大规模的公园（奎尔公园），还有奎尔的墓地。

高迪像其他艺术家一样从大自然中寻找创作灵感，大自然就是他的灵感缪斯，但极少会有人把树木、水果篮、蜥蜴、鱼骨等形状用到建筑的架构中去。例如，在圣家族教堂的尖塔上，有着巨大的水果篮雕塑。高迪说，大自然“是一本伟大的书，它向我们敞开，而我们也应该要求自己去阅读它”。对高迪来说，建筑的形式和图案，以及他常常运用的色彩，都是从大自然中汲取的灵感。为了表现大自然中无限的色彩，他甚至发明了一个名为“瓷砖拼贴法”的建筑做法，将瓷砖、瓶子和瓷器打碎，作为小瓷砖，来制造抽象的马赛克图案。

1883年，高迪开始他的杰作圣家族教堂的修建工作。然而，最初用于教堂建设的大量资助，在世纪之交时就完全告终了，高迪不得不卖掉自己的房子，甚至在街角乞讨来筹集资金。晚年时的高迪身体每况愈下，他搬去圣家族教堂以离自己的“神殿”更近，并在那里度过了自己的余生。直到他去世，那座已经动工了43年的教堂，只完成了15%。

冲突的艺术视觉和烦琐的财政问题，也成为许多希望帮助高迪完成圣家族教堂的人的痛苦之源。在高迪去世之后，政客和建筑家针对其他建筑家是否能公正完好地完成高迪的设计展开了激烈的讨论。最终，大多数人达成如下共识：高迪留下的蓝图和计划，足以清晰地反映他的设计。但不幸的是，高迪的墓地、工作间和所有遗留下来的设计作品都被西班牙内战期间的炸弹摧毁了。20世纪50年代，教堂的建设工作慢慢恢复，虽然这时已经有了比原来更多的资金，但没有什么大的进展。直到80年代，稳定的资助才使得教堂的修建工作取得明显的进展。不过，要完成高迪的设计仍然需要至少30年的时间。并且，人们常抱怨说现代建筑师毁坏了高迪设计的纯粹性，这种情况也是有可能的。

在最近几十年里，艺术界经历了一场革新，艺术家们开始以一种全新的视角审视和评价被称为“新艺术”的艺术作品。作为最著名的新艺术建筑师，高迪备受赞誉。巴塞罗那宣布2002年为“高迪年”，并举办了30多场展览和活动来向他致敬。同时，那些以前不对外开放的建筑，第一次向公众敞开大门。九万多人聚集在圣家族教堂前，庆祝高迪的150岁诞辰。

对于人们的认可，高迪很可能是赞同的。因为他从未怀疑过自己创造力的天赋，也从不允许自己的助手质疑他。不管评论家对他多么苛责，他始终坚持自己独特的设计。如今，评论家们看到了高迪的才华。在历经了建筑界功能设计的几十年后，高迪如艺术品般的建筑设计更受欢迎。正如现代建筑师诺曼·福斯特所断言的，“高迪的设计理念，即便是在一个世纪之后，依然是革命性的”。毋庸置疑，高迪天才般的建筑风格将会永远流传下去。

Gaudi, the Genius Architect

Most of the world's great cathedrals are impressive in their size and beauty, but the Sagrada Familia stands apart even from these architectural masterpieces because of its unique and startling design. This stunning cathedral towers above Barcelona like a strange, ornate sandcastle. With bright carving of fruit baskets, a central nave that mirrors a forest of trees, bizarre spires, and beautiful spiral staircases, the iconic Sagrada Familia has become as well-known as the Eiffel Tower or Statue of Liberty. Moreover, the Safrada Familia captures the "freakish genius" of its designer Antoni Gaudi better than any of his other creations.

Today, crowds flock to Barcelona to witness Gaudi's great works, including Casa Mila, Casa Battlo, Palau Güell, Park Güell, and, of course, the Sagrada Familia. However, the current popularity of Gaudi's work would not have been foreseen when he first unveiled his creations. Critics of his time described his work as hideous and compared his buildings to monsters or dungeons; as recently as 50 years ago, the so-called genius of Gaudi was not well-recognized.

Antoni Gaudi I Cornet was born in 1852 to a family of artisans in a small town in northern Spain. When he was 16, he moved to Barcelona to finish his secondary education and study architecture. Even at this early age, he engendered controversy: often truant from class, he criticized the standard architectural education of the day and complained that his classes were devoid of creativity. Ultimately, he was granted a degree, but just barely. His school director insightfully commented that Gaudi was either "a genius or a madman."

After graduation, Gaudi remained in Barcelona. The city was growing, and rich benefactors were looking for artists to design modern, trendy buildings. In his mid-twenties, Gaudi met his lifelong patron Eusebi Güell, a wealthy industrialist and politician. For almost four decades, Güell would fund Gaudi's work for a wide array of venues, from Güell's private mansion (the Palau Güell) to a massive public park (Park Güell) to the Güell's own crypt.

Nature was Gaudi's muse; many artists find inspiration in nature as he did, but few actually carved shapes found in nature such as trees, fruit baskets, lizards, and bones into the physical architecture of his buildings. For example, the Sagrada Familia has huge carvings of fruit baskets amid its spires. Gaudi said that nature was "the Great Book, always open, that we should force ourselves to read." For Gaudi, nature was inspiration for the forms and motifs of his buildings and for the colors he used liberally. In order to represent the limitless diversity of colors found in nature, he even forged a new architectural practice known as trencadis, in which tiles, bottles, and pottery were smashed into small tiles to create abstract mosaics.

In 1883, Gaudi began work on his masterpiece, the Sagrada Familia. However, when the initial and substantial financial contributions for the church's construction fizzled out completely around the turn of the century, Gaudi had to sell his own home and even beg on street corners to raise funds. As his health declined in later years, Gaudi moved into the Sagrada Familia to be closer to "his temple" and remained there for the rest of his life. At the time of his death, forty-three years after construction began, the church was only 15 percent complete.

Conflicting artistic vision and pesky finances have been the source of much grief for those who have hoped to finish Gaudi's vision for the Sagrada Familia. After his death, politicians and architects clashed over whether other architects would be able to do his design justice. Eventually, the major players agreed that the blueprints and plans Gaudi left behind would be sufficient to achieve his vision; unfortunately, bombing during the Spanish Civil War destroyed Gaudi's crypt, workroom, and all the remaining designs. Construction on the church slowly resumed in the mid-1950s, in part due to a lot more funding than in the past, but little progress was made until the 1980s, when steady donations began funding significant progress. However, the church will still take at least another three decades to realize Gaudi's complete design. It is likely, moreover, that there will always be grumblings that modern architects ruined the purity of Gaudi's design.

In recent decades, the art world has experienced a renewed appreciation of the style known as Art Nuevo. As the most famous of all Art. Nuevo architects, Gaudi has been showered with acclaim. In fact, Barcelona declared 2002 the Year of Gaudi and held over 30 exhibitions and events in his honor. Buildings that had previously been closed to the public were opened for the first time, and over 90,000 people gathered in front of the Sagrada Familia to celebrate the 150th anniversary of Gaudi's birth.

Gaudi would most likely approve of such recognition. He never doubted his creative genius, did not allow his assistants to question him, and persevered with his fanciful designs despite harsh reviews by critics of his day. Current critics, however, see the gift of Gaudi as clearly as he did at the time. After decades of functional designs in the architectural world, Gaudi's architecture-as-art is once more popular. As modern architect Norman Foster asserts, "Gaudi's methods, one century on, continue to be revolutionary." His genius is and will continue to be undisputed.

专注成就天才
A Focused Intelligence

飞行员查尔斯·A.林德伯格无疑是个天才。1927年，他成为第一个完成从纽约到巴黎单人不着陆飞行的人。如此巨大的成功不是单单因为专业技术水平的高超，更是其超凡智慧和坚定决心的结晶。

在童年和青年时期，查尔斯·林德伯格对读书没有表现出过多的兴趣。1918年，美国参与第一次世界大战期间，林德伯格急切地同意回到家里的农场上为参战军队种植粮食，以换取自己的高中毕业证书。虽然这个位于明尼苏达州的小农场在他的精心照料下获得大丰收，但是农场并不是他的兴趣所在。他真正感兴趣的是机械。当他把自己的爱好告诉父母后，身为国会议员的父亲和作为教师的母亲鼓励他去接受更为正规的教育。

林德伯格来到威斯康星大学学习机械工程。但是仅仅两年后，由于对动手实践的强烈兴趣，加之缺乏专业知识背景和学习技巧，他就收到学校留校察看的通知。当林德伯格意识到自己在大学所学的那点儿知识足够让他参加美国预备役军官训练营后，他就选择了退学，以后再也没有回来继续完成大学学业。

1922年，在内布拉斯加飞机公司接受短期的飞行训练后，林德伯格用了两年的时间奔走各地，做过演说家、机翼行走者、跳伞者以及特技跳伞运动员。当他发现自己真正的兴趣是飞行员后，他和103名军校生一起应征入伍，参加了飞行训练班。

虽然讨厌课堂学习，但林德伯格还是专心致志，潜心学习各种飞行知识。只要任何一项测试不合格，就将被淘汰出局。但是林德伯格以优异的成绩通过了所有的测试。1925年，林德伯格以全班第一名的成绩毕业，毕业时和他同期进入训练班的军校生只剩下18名。

虽然对正规教育兴趣不大，但是林德伯格终其一生都在享受学习的乐趣，并不断寻找和接受新的挑战。他绘制的跨洲越洋航线被沿用至今。他嫂子严重的心脏病促使他和外科医生亚历克西斯·卡雷尔展开合作，研制出灌注泵装置。这种装置可以保存受损心脏，保证其在接受医生的修复手术时能够继续跳动。如果查尔斯·林德伯格回顾其丰富的充满智慧的一生，就会明白他将自己的智慧集中在不同寻常的道路上，并改变了这个世界。

A Focused Intelligence

Aviator Charles A. Lindbergh was undeniably a man of genius. In 1927, he was the first person to complete a successful flight from New York to Paris. Such success was not the result of academic excellence, but the result, of ingenuity and determination.

Throughout his childhood and early adulthood, Charles Lindbergh was not interested in erudition. In 1918, with the United States in the throes of World War I, Lindbergh eagerly agreed to return to the family farm to grow food for the war effort in exchange for his high school diploma. Though the small Minnesota farm thrived under his care, his passion was not for agriculture, but for things mechanical. When he expressed these interests to his parents, a congressman and a teacher, they encouraged him to obtain a more formal education.

Lindbergh attended the University of Wisconsin to study engineering. However, Lindbergh's penchant for "hands-on" learning, combined with a lack of scholarly discipline and study skills, resulted in academic probation after barely two years. Realizing that the only practical knowledge he had gained in college was through his participation in the Reserve Officers' Training Corps (R.O.T.C.), Lindbergh dropped out of college, never to return.

In 1922, after brief aviation training at the Nebraska Aircraft Corporation, Lindbergh spent two summers traveling from state to state, performing as a barnstormer, wing walker, parachutist, and skydiver. Having found his true passion as a pilot, Lindbergh enlisted in the Army along with 103 other cadets.

Despite his aversion to classroom learning, he focused his efforts and learned to truly study during ground school. Failing any one test would have resulted in being "washed out," but Lindbergh passed his tests with "flying" colors. When he graduated in 1925, only eighteen cadets remained, and Lindbergh achieved the highest ranking among all of the members of his class.

Despite his disinterest in formal education, Lindbergh displayed an enjoyment of learning throughout his life, seeking out and accepting new challenges. He charted transcontinental and transoceanic air routes that are still used today. His sister-in-law's fatal heart condition led to his work with surgeon Alexis Carrel in developing a perfusion pump, which enabled a damaged heart to continue pumping while doctors worked to repair it. Charles Lindbergh could look back with the wisdom of life's experiences, knowing that he had focused his intelligence in untraditional ways and changed the world.

丰富美国文化
Enriching the American Tradition

充满诸多冲突与妥协的美墨战争，代表了美国一部分被忽视的历史，但是它的重要性在美国当地文化中也不能被夸大。确实，很难想象现在的美国没有之前属于墨西哥的那部分领土（包括得克萨斯州、亚利桑那州、加利福尼亚州和其他地区）会是什么样的，同样很难想象，如今美国充满活力的多元社会如果没有美籍墨西哥人的影响的话，会是什么样子。

尽管美籍墨西哥人在丰富美国文化方面做出了很多贡献，他们在文学方面的贡献却常常被忽视。尽管美籍墨西哥人的名字经常出现在电影和音乐中，但许多美国人压根说不出一位美籍墨西哥作家的名字。

作家瑞兹得伯顿于1885年发表了她的第二部小说《棚户区先生》，从而成为早期美籍墨西哥文学上的一个重要里程碑。这部小说不仅是第一部由墨西哥血统的作者用英语写的小说，而且小说中对革命的看法也尤其引人注意。通过小说中的家庭阿拉玛家，作者向美国读者们介绍了一个他们还不太熟悉的群体。阿拉玛家原是生活在圣地亚哥的一个拥有土地的乡绅家庭，但在美墨战争中，美国吞并加利福尼亚州之后，阿拉玛家几乎失去了一切。由于不平等的《瓜瓦卢佩·伊达尔戈条约》，墨西哥失去了约40%的领土，而且有很多像瑞兹得伯顿和她笔下的阿拉玛家族一样的人，不得不背井离乡，远离原本舒适的生活，变成了一个新的国家的公民。瑞兹得伯顿希望通过她的作品，讲出许多美籍墨西哥人共同的忧虑。《棚户区先生》是美籍墨西哥文学探索过程早期的一个重要标志，它也激励着更多的美籍墨西哥作家继续探索，在人性、身份认同以及个人和集体历史的关系等主题上，不断开拓。

直到今天，瑞兹得伯顿和其他美籍墨西哥作者的作品，依然是美国文学重要的一部分。1977年以来，诗人安娜·卡斯蒂洛出版了许多广受欢迎的小说和诗集，她的作品让更多的人了解到美籍墨西哥妇女的困境，尤其是那些住在像卡斯蒂洛的家乡芝加哥这样的城市的妇女。桑德拉·西斯内罗斯的《芒果街上的小屋》，自1984年出版以来，已经卖出了200万册。她的作品，包括2002年出版的小说《卡拉米洛》，说出了经常身陷两种文化困境中的美籍墨西哥人的心声。和许多人一起，这些作家们继续壮大着美国文学，就像遍布全国的美籍墨西哥人都在努力丰富和挑战既定概念的“美国文化”那样。

Enriching the American Tradition

The Mexican-American War, with its many conflicts and compromises, represents a largely overlooked part of the history of the United States, but its importance in the current shape and culture of the United States cannot be overstated. Certainly, it is difficult to imagine the present-day United States without the list of former Mexican territories, which includes Texas, Arizona, California, and others, but it is equally difficult to imagine America's vibrant multicultural society without the influence of Mexican-Americans.

But despite the obvious richness that Mexican—Americans have brought to American culture, one aspect of their contributions to American arts is often overlooked: literature. Although the names of many famous Mexican-Americans are identifiable in film and music, many Americans are at a loss to name even a single Mexican-American author.

A major landmark in early Mexican-American literature came in 1885, when author María Amparo Ruiz de Burton, published her second novel, *The Squatter and the Don*. In addition to being the first major novel written in English by an author of Mexican descent, *The Squatter and the Don* was also noteworthy for its revolutionary perspective. María Amparo Ruiz de Burton helped to introduce American readers to an as yet unfamiliar group through her fictional family, the Alamars. A family of landed gentry living in San Diego, the Alamars lose nearly all that they own after the American annexation of California during the Mexican–American War. As a result of the lopsided Treaty of Guadalupe Hidalgo, Mexico lost nearly forty percent of its previous territories and many, like Ruiz de Burton and her creations the Alamars, were uprooted from their previous comfort and made citizens of a new nation. Ruiz de Burton's wish was that her works would speak for the many Mexican–Americans who felt the same concerns. *The Squatter and the Don* marked an early and important exploration of many themes that Mexican–American authors continue to explore, including themes of personal integrity, identity, and the relationships between individuals and collective history.

Ruiz de Burton's writings and those of other authors remain important parts of American literature today. Poet Ana Castillo has been publishing well–received novels and volumes of poetry prolifically since 1977, and her work has been essential in bringing issues of Mexican–American women, particularly those living in urban places such as Castillo's hometown of Chicago, to a larger audience. Sandra Cisneros is the author of *The House on Mango Street*, which has sold over two million copies since its original publication in 1984, and her work, including the novel *Caramelo*, published in 2002, has helped give voice to the often difficult position of living between two cultures that Mexican-Americans face. Along with many others, these authors continue to expand the boundaries of American literature, just as Mexican-Americans all over the country continue to enrich and challenge accepted notions of what we call "American culture."

杰基·罗宾森：不只是一名棒球手
Jackie Robinson: More than a Ballplayer

当美国恢复每年春天的棒球赛后，人们总会在四月的一天纪念杰基·罗宾森，这个人打破了美国体育运动中肤色的限制。他在棒球场取得了诸多佳绩，给人留下了非常深刻的印象，而他在民权运动中做出的贡献——用他的遗孀瑞秋·罗宾森的话来说——和棒球同等重要，却往往被忽视。

杰基·罗宾森在布鲁克林道奇队效力时英勇顽强的比赛风格，也是他专注民权运动的一种反映。从让他这个非洲裔美国人进入棒球队这个“伟大实验”开始，他就明白，自己的表现将会成为解决体育界种族隔离问题的一个重要因素。杰基将观众们对他的反应渐渐地从嘲笑、骚扰转变为欢呼和接受，因为体育场上在座的每一位白人观众，都能从他身上看到巨大的才能。场上和场下的成功，让杰基成为一位受人尊敬的人物，而一直以来，杰基都以克制的态度来面对人们对他的偏见。

杰基花费大量精力用来躲避各种潜在的陷害，换作其他人的话，恐怕早已经变得日渐憔悴，甚至一蹶不振，但是杰基却出于本能地，不屈不挠地努力着，一直致力于体育界和非裔美国人社区的民权运动。今天，许多运动员用他们在体育界取得的地位来换取名利，杰基却不断用自己的地位来推动民权运动的进步。他经常利用棒球比赛的机会，在美国各地进行演讲，呼吁人们结束种族隔离，捍卫自己的权利。

退役之后，杰基成为一名企业家，但是他不忘初心，一有时间就给总统写信或发电报，字里行间充满激情。他用自己在体育界取得的地位敦促总统也能像他一样关注民权运动。

尽管比起在民权运动上的不懈努力，杰基在棒球上的成绩更加为人所知，但他在棒球场上表现出的惊人的勇气，恰恰反映了他反对种族隔离和不平等待遇的坚定立场。他的众多反对者也一再发现，杰基不但从没有气馁，反而更加努力。最后，民权运动终于出现了转机，胜利的火花被点燃，杰基将民权运动的火花燃为火炬，并终其一生，一直传递着人人平等的理念和思想。

Jackie Robinson: More than a Ballplayer

When baseball resumes in America every spring, one April day is always reserved to honor Jackie Robinson, the man who broke the color barrier of America's national pastime. While his accomplishments on the baseball field were numerous and impressive, his civil rights activism was, according to his widow Rachel Robinson, equally important and often overlooked.

The tenacious and spirited way Jackie Robinson played baseball for the Brooklyn Dodgers was a reflection of his focus on civil rights. Form the outset of the "Great Experiment" of having African-Americans in baseball, he knew that his performance on the field would be a determining factor in sports segregation. Jackie gradually converted jeers and harassment into cheers and acceptance because white spectators could see his immense talent from any seat in the stadium. Jackie became a highly respected figure by continually succeeding on and off the field, all the while displaying stoic restraint in the face of initial prejudice.

The vast amount of energy Jackie expended avoiding a myriad of potential pitfalls could have caused any man to wilt; rather, he instinctively and relentlessly increased his efforts for positive civil rights changes, both in his sport and in the African-American community at large. While many athletes today use their status to garner endorsements and live as celebrities,

Jackie constantly utilized his status to stimulate civil rights advancements. He often used his baseball travels as opportunities to speak publicly to blacks in U.S. cities about ending segregation and vigilantly defending their rights.

Post–baseball, Jackie became an entrepreneur, but his focus did not stray as he found time to write impassioned letters and telegrams to various U.S. presidents during the civil rights movement. He had the status to demand that they too remain firmly focused on civil rights measures.

Though Jackie Robinson's baseball exploits may be more widely known than his tireless efforts in the civil rights movement, his astonishing courage on the baseball field was itself a resounding stance against segregation and inequality. His numerous detractors consistently found that not only was Jackie undeterred, but he was excelling in his efforts. As a result, the spark of positive change was ignited. Jackie turned that spark for civil rights into a torch and carried it his entire life.

切斯纳特的文学生涯

Conjuring a Prophetic Literary Career

作家、评论家查尔斯·W.切斯纳特于1858年在俄亥俄州出生。他的青少年时期正值美国的重建阶段，当时他大部分时间都是在北卡罗莱纳州度过的。虽然他的父母都是自由的非裔美国人，但切斯纳特强烈地感受到了非裔美国人在内战结束后那段时间在美国国土上的挣扎。经历了南方动乱的切斯纳特开始在文学中寻找慰藉，在他十几岁的时候，他就已经下定决心成为一位作家。

1887年，他的作品《被糟蹋的葡萄藤》在美国《大西洋月刊》上发表，这是切斯纳特在文学上取得的首次成功。这次成功激励着切斯纳特书写更多的故事，最后这些故事被整理成一本小说集，在1889年以《女人的召唤》为名而出版。《女人的召唤》传承了早期民俗研究者乔尔·钱德勒·哈里斯和托马斯·尼尔森·佩吉的写作风格。但是，这本书更加直接和诚实地提出了奴隶时期及重建时期南方地区的种族关系。《女人的召唤》以及故事的讲述者朱利叶斯·麦卡度叔叔，显然是对哈里斯的故事中特别受欢迎的雷穆斯叔叔的一种回敬，但这两者之间的相似性也就到此为止了。与哈里斯故事中的贝尔兔和其他小动物不同，《女人的召唤》充满了各种巫术和神秘色彩，而且它是用人物角色来讲述不公正的奴隶制度。

不过，切斯纳特真正的杰作是《雪松后的房子》。这部小说讲述了在一个非裔美国家庭里，孩子希望能把自己变成白人的故事，这也是涉及这一题材的早期小说之一。切斯纳特使用角色分裂的身份，在南方的黑人和白人世界中来回穿梭，在这个过程中，他成功地展示了两个世界间的惊人差距，以及他笔下的角色和在现实生活中把自己变成白人的黑人所遇到的难以克服的困境。从1900年出版起，这部小说就在美国文学界引起了巨大的轰动，同时获得了尊重与美誉，例如著名的白人文学评论家威廉·迪恩·豪威尔斯以及黑人知识分子杜布瓦，都对它有颇高的评价。

尽管切斯纳特持续写作到1932年去世，但很明显，他在《雪松后的房子》和《一脉相承》（1901）之后的作品，对于当时的美国社会来说，太过于具有煽动性。当时的美国，种族关系的话题一旦被提出，就会让人感到不安，更何况像切斯纳特这样的作家竟敢公然讨论这一话题呢。但是，在最近几年中，切斯纳特的声誉得到了恢复，而且被视为先锋人物。今天，正如在19世纪末期一样，切斯纳特的作品不仅为我们提供了大量文学杰作，更为我们了解美国种族关系问题提供了有力和预见性的视角。

切斯纳特既是作家又是评论家，他是美国黑人文学的先锋。他的小说和故事自出版之日起，就具有十分重大的意义，时至今日，依然如此。

Conjuring a Prophetic Literary Career

Born in Ohio in 1858, Charles W. Chesnutt was an author and essayist who, during the Reconstruction era, spent much of his youth in North Carolina. Though his parents were free African-Americans, Chesnutt felt intensely the struggles of African-Americans in the United States in the period directly after the Civil War. Amid all the turmoil of the South of his boyhood, Chesnutt took solace in literature, and he had already decided, in his teens, that he would become a writer.

The Goophered Grapevine, published in 1887 in *The Atlantic*, was Chesnutt's first major literary success, and this success encouraged Chesnutt to publish additional tales, which were eventually collected in *The Conjure Woman (1899)*. *The Conjure Woman* was written in the tradition of earlier folklorists Joel Chandler Harris and Thomas Nelson Page, however, it presented a much more frank treatment of race relations in the South during slavery and Reconstruction. *The Conjure Woman* and its narrator, Uncle Julius McAdoo, were clearly written in response to the immensely popular Uncle Remus of Harris's tales, but the similarities between the two authors' works ended there. In the place of Brer Rabbit and the animal from Harris's tales, *The Conjure Woman* used human characters in stories that incorporated conjure, voodoo, and the injustices of slavery.

Chesnutt's true masterpiece, however, is *The House Behind the Cedars*. The novel details the lives of an African–American family's children who have chosen to "pass" as white, making *The House Behind the Cedars* one of the first novels to talk about racial passing. Chesnutt uses his characters' divided status to travel back and forth between the black and white worlds of the South, and in the process, Chesnutt manages to show both the shocking disparity between the two worlds and the insurmountable difficulties his characters, and those who "pass" in real life, face. From the moment it was published in 1900, the novel was a sensation in American letters, garnering the respect and admiration of such prominent white literary critics as William Dean Howells and black intellectuals such as W.E.B. Dubois.

Although Chesnutt continued to write until his death in 1932, it had become clear that the work he completed after *The House Behind* the Cedars and *The Marrow of Tradition* (1901) had become too inflammatory to a society ever uneasy about the topic of race relations in the United States, particularly when authors had brought these problems as close to the surface as Chesnutt had. In recent years, however, Chesnutt's reputation has been restored and he has been treated as the pioneer that he most certainly was. Today as much as in the late nineteenth century, Chesnutt's works provide us with a number of literary masterpieces and a powerful and prophetic vision of race relations in the United States.

Both author and essayist, Charles W. Chesnutt was a pioneer in African-American literature whose novels and tales are as meaningful today as they were when first published.

【第三章】
NO.3

味蕾主义

Fine Food

世界语文·美国语文
International Literature American Literature
2

烹饪
Cooking

在很小的时候，我就对烹饪产生了浓厚的兴趣。那个时候，大家认为烹饪是个很适合小女孩的兴趣，而我又是家里六个孩子之中唯一的女孩子，于是妈妈积极鼓励我发掘对烹饪的好奇心。不过，没人想到我会以烹饪为职业。不管怎么说，在我高中毕业之前，我的厨艺按美国的标准来说已经算非常好了。在家的时候，大部分时间都是我负责做饭，我还把自制的蛋糕、曲奇和面包卖给邻居。我在二手书店买了一些带有插图的欧洲杂志，在学校学的法语足够让我看懂那些杂志里刊登的文章和菜谱。我敢说在我以前还没有人在新汉普郡出售过牛角面包。当然了，现在你可以在任何一家出售沃登面包的店里买到牛角面包。

在我上大学头两年，做饭多多少少退出了我的生活。我上的是一所女子大学，我们统一吃学校食堂的饭菜。虽然餐厅布局优雅，桌子上都铺着一尘不染的亚麻布，不过团体膳食的饭菜味道真是太可怕了。大三的时候，我住在一小间学生宿舍里。当时学校职工因为薪酬太低，正在举行罢工。所以我们不得不一起分担宿舍的日常事务。我主动要求负责做饭。其实这和在家里做饭没什么两样，因为我们可是有一大家子人呢。和学校的厨师一比，我简直就是大厨艾斯可菲。我对那些新鲜蔬菜的兴趣可比对俄国历史的兴趣大得多；我解决营养问题可比做数学题的时候用心多了。为此，我的学习成绩出现了严重下滑。

我的室友南希是一个傲慢的女孩，来自伦敦一个很富有的家庭。罢工开始之前，她几乎没有跟我说过话。南希钟情美味的食物。上大学以后，一直吃那些倒胃口的饭菜，我负责做饭后，她才开始对饭菜有所期待。她对烹饪的知识比我见过的任何人都多。后来我知道，她家在纽约经营着一家豪华酒店、一家意大利餐厅和一家法国餐厅。我们很快成了好朋友。她有个疯狂的想法，就是将来自己经营家族企业。在那个年头，这个想法跟女人去当飞行员、大学校长或者最高法院的法官一样荒唐。她还说将来我一定能成为这座城市最好的厨师。

Cooking

Even as a small child, I was interested in cooking. My mother encouraged my curiosity, since in those days cooking was thought to be a suitable interest for a little girl, and I was the only daughter among six children. Not, of course, that anyone ever imagined I would cook professionally. Anyway, before I had graduated from high school, I was very good by American standards. I did most of the cooking at home and sold my cakes, cookies, and breads to neighbors. I had learned enough French in school to be able to make my way through the articles and recipes I found in the illustrated European magazines I bought at the second-hand book shops. I'm certain that mine were the first croissants ever put on sale in New Hampshire, though nowadays you can buy them in any store that sells Wonder Bread.

In my first two years of college, cooking more or less slipped my mind. I went to a women's college, where we all ate the appalling institutional food in elegant dining rooms with spotless linen on the tables. In my junior year, I was living in a small dorm when the college workers—they were criminally underpaid—went out on strike. We divided up the chores in the dorm, and I volunteered to cook the dinners. It was really not greatly different from cooking for my large family. Compared to the college cooks,

I looked like Escoffier. My studies slipped badly because I was clearly more interested in crisp vegetables than in Russian history and more engaged by the problems of nutrition than by the problems of mathematics.

One of the other residents of my dorm was a rich, rather snooty girl from New York who had hardly spoken to me before the strike. Nancy loved good food, and for the first time since she came to college could now actually look forward to dinner. She knew more about cooking than anyone I had ever met. It turned out that her family owned a posh hotel and an Italian and a French restaurant in New York City. We were soon best friends. She had a crazy idea of running the family business herself, in those days as likely as a woman astronaut, college president, or Supreme Court justice. And she said that I was to become the best chef in the city.

好侍者，好顾客

Good Waiter, Good Customer

一年多以来，为了帮家里分担自己的教育费用，我一直在一家餐厅做服务员。服务员的工作本就不好做，再加上现在的好顾客少之又少，这份工作做起来就更加不易。对于一名服务员来说，好顾客的标准包括：彬彬有礼、体贴他人、善解人意。这些标准其实也正是用餐者对好侍者的期待。顾客和服务员之间应该是种互惠的关系。

在餐厅繁忙的时候，好顾客应该做好稍等一会儿的心理准备。他们应该在开始点餐时就讲清楚自己的需要，而不是一会儿说想要牛排里放些蘑菇，一会儿要沙拉调味料放在一边，或者一会儿又要全熟的汉堡，以免去服务员来回奔波之苦。如果某位顾客没把需要讲清楚，让服务员跑来跑去的话，结果就会导致这名服务员不能够及时为其负责的其他顾客提供服务。

如果服务员告诉用餐者火鸡汉堡需要较长一点儿时间才能做好，好顾客会用心听取服务员的解释和说明，不会在用餐时反复呼喊服务员："为什么我们的火鸡汉堡还没有做好？"如果服务员告诉顾客今天的辣椒特别辣，好顾客就不会再点辣椒，不会在发现自己矫情的胃承受不了时要求把辣椒退掉。

许多餐厅会训练自己的员工向顾客推销某种食品或饮料，这些东西一般利润比较大或者供给过多。好顾客应该在服务员推销的时候耐心一点儿，毕竟这是服务员工作的一部分。而在推销的时候，服务员要尽量让自己的介绍听起来生动有趣，哪怕这些内容他一天之内已经说了30次之多。

尽管顾客给的小费丰厚时，服务员或许会原谅他们的粗鲁，尽管遇到体贴周到的顾客却分文小费不给的时候，服务员会愤愤不平，好服务员看重的远不止小费的多寡。如果一份工作除了金钱之外，不能提供别的回报，那么这份工作也会让人心生不满。如果一名服务员不喜欢自己的工作，那么他就会把这种不满情绪传递给他的顾客。闹情绪的服务员会导致顾客不满意，如果不满意的顾客太多，那么这名服务员很快就要被炒鱿鱼了。

Good Waiter, Good Customer

For more than a year, I have helped to pay for my education by working as a waiter. It is not an easy job, and it is made harder by the scarcity of good clients. To a waiter, a good client is a customer who is well-mannered, thoughtful, and sensitive, the same qualities a diner looks for in a good waiter. The patron-waiter relationship should be reciprocal.

Good clients should be prepared to wait a little longer if a restaurant is very busy. They should be prepared to make all their needs clear from the beginning so the waiter doesn't have to make extra trips when they forget to say they want mushrooms with their steak, salad dressing on the side, and a hamburger well done. Extra trips to one table will slow down the service at all the other tables at a waiter's station.

Good customers listen when the waiter explains that the turkey burger takes longer to cook and don't keep calling the waiter over to ask why it is taking so long. If the waiter tells them the chili is very spicy today, they don't order the chili and send it back when they find out it's too hot for their delicate stomachs.

Many restaurants train their staff to try to sell certain foods or drinks, usually those that produce more profit or are in over supply. Customers should be patient with a sales pitch, since it is part of a waiter's job. At the same time, waiters must try to sound interested, even though they are saying something they have said thirty times that day.

Though probably willing to forgive some rudeness if the tip is large, and resentful of even the most thoughtful customer who leaves no tip at all, good waiters think about more than the size of the tips. Any regular job that has no rewards except money eventually becomes unsatisfying, and waiters who dislike their jobs will, in time, communicate their discontent to their customers. Sullen waiters will soon have unhappy clients.

比尔·威廉姆斯使美国家庭共进晚餐

Bill Williams Brings America Home to Dinner

美国有家叫作“荣耀食品”的公司，其经营标语是“只有最好”。如果你对这家公司有一定的了解，你不得不欣赏这家公司的诚实。比尔·威廉姆斯是公司的董事长，也是公司的创始人。他对公司的标语曾作过这样的解释：“尽管我们的食物不能与家里厨房做的美味媲美，但它们却非常接近。”

在比尔·威廉姆斯很小的时候，他就喜欢为家人准备美味的食物。当他长大成人以后，曾在美国知名烹饪学院进修，学到了精湛的烹饪技术。1989年，他突然有了开设南方料理连锁店的想法。当时美国还没有人专门经营为非裔美国人提供食物的快餐店。在接下来的三年内，他研发出一系列特色食品，包括罐头蔬菜、罐头甘薯、罐头菜豆、罐头秋葵，还有瓶装的辣椒酱和玉米面包等。

最后，威廉姆斯准备从杂货店开始出售自己的食物。1922年，荣耀食品第一次出现在俄亥俄州的食品店里。紧接着，它很快就占领了邻近的其他几个州的市场。一年内，其销售量就比原来预想的多了一倍。

公司以非裔美籍人为主要销售对象。这一点通过公司提供的荣耀食品就不难看出。公司总部就处于威廉姆斯小时候居住过且在那里长大的黑人街区。公司为当地几家社区项目提供资金支持。只要可能，公司就会雇佣非裔美国专业顾问和转包商，并且公司已经与非裔美国农民签订了合同，种植很多荣耀食物所需的作物和蔬菜。

公司的名称同样反映了以非裔美国人为重点的经营模式。荣耀容易让人想到福音教堂的欢跃精神，以及讲述内战期间黑色军团故事的电影。这部电影同样以“荣耀”为名。

“荣耀食品”公司从成立初到现在已经走过了很长一段路，从某种意义上讲，美国人晚上可以和家人一起共进晚餐要多亏比尔·威廉姆斯的努力、坚持和高超的烹饪技术。

Bill Williams Brings America Home to Dinner

You have to admire the honesty of a company whose slogan is "Just About the Best." Glory Foods' president and founder, Bill Williams, explains the unusual slogan by admitting that while he knows that his food can't beat the taste of real home cooking, they do come very close.

Even as a child, Williams loved to prepare food, and as a young adult, he refined his cooking skills at the prestigious Culinary Institute of America. He came up with his idea for a line of Southern-inspired cuisine in 1989, a time when there were no convenience foods designed for African American consumers. Over the next three years, he developed a line of products that included canned greens, sweet potatoes, beans, and okra, as well as bottled hot sauce and cornbread mixes.

Eventually, Williams was ready to launch his products in grocery stores. Glory Foods were first offered for sale in Ohio in 1992 and soon became available in neighboring states. Within a year, sales were twice the original projections.

The company's African American focus is evident in all aspects of Glory Foods. The firm's headquarters are located in the same black neighborhood where Williams grew up, and the company helps to support several local community projects. The firm also employs African American professional adversers and subcontractors whenever possible and contracts African American farmers to grow much of the produce that goes into Glory Foods.

The company's name reflects this African American focus as well. Glory is mean to evoke both the exultant spirit of gospel churches and the movie of the same name, which tells the story of a black regiment during the Civil War.

Glory Foods has come a long way from its beginnings. America's dinner tables are the beneficiaries of Bill William's drive, determination, and culinary expertise.

成为一名法国大厨
Becoming A French Chef

为什么法国的美食在全世界都享有盛名？部分答案就是法国的饮食文化历史悠久，食客们对饮食又非常挑剔。他们还有新鲜优质的水果、蔬菜、肉类和鱼类。不过，最关键的一点是法国厨师的培训方式。在法国，厨师是很受人尊敬的职业，就像美国的医生或律师一样。虽然大部分的美国厨师都是在本土接受的培训，但是一些立志成为大厨的美国人会到法国学习厨艺。最受尊崇的几所烹饪学校都在法国的首都巴黎。这些学校都有五十多年的历史了。不过大部分的美国人会选择诸如蓝带这样讲英语的学校。

立志成为厨师的人，一般在很小的时候就开始接受厨师培训。刚开始的时候，他们需要学习两三年的基本功和做学徒工。在法国的学徒和美国的实习生可不一样。学徒制的历史可以追溯到中世纪。学徒的工作很辛苦，也很枯燥乏味，比如给堆积如山的蔬菜削皮，清洗数不完的锅碗瓢盆和其他炊具。一般而言，一名学徒每天要在厨房工作十一个小时，学徒的工资很低，工作时间又长，但是有机会看到主厨是怎么工作的，所有这些辛苦也值了。

学徒每天要工作很长时间，这需要很好的体力才行。这也许就是法国男厨师的数量要远远多于女厨师的原因。学徒期满后，就要开始专门的训练，比如做点心或餐后甜点。法国厨师有五个不同层次的资格认证，这和美国大学的学位制很像。就像奥林匹克运动会一样，法国每三年会举行一次厨师大赛，胜出者有资格在其姓名后加上M.O.F.（法国最优秀职人）这三个字母，并且很可能会名声大噪。

Becoming A French Chef

Why is French cooking so famous? Some answers are that they have a long history of good eating and eaters who are fussy. They also have wonderful fresh fruits, vegetables, meats and fish. But the key is the way chefs in France are trained. In France, a chef is looked up to and respected like a doctor or lawyer in the U.S.A. Some Americans who want to become chefs go to France to learn. But a far larger number of American cooks are trained in the United States. The most respected cooking schools in France are in the capital, Paris. They have been in operation for more than fifty years. But most American students go to schools like the Cordon Blue where they speak English.

In France, training begins at a young age. There are, to begin, two or three years of technical study and apprentice work. An apprenticeship in France is not like an internship in the U.S. Apprenticeships descend from a system that dates back to the middle ages. The work is very hard and boring, like peeling huge piles of vegetables or washing pots and pans and kitchen utensils. An apprentice in a French kitchen usually works eleven hours each day. The pay is small, and the hours are long, but the chance to watch a master chef at work is worth it.

Chefs in training work long hours, requiring great physical strength.

This is the reason, perhaps, far more chefs are men than women in France. A next step after apprenticeship might be learning a specialty, like making pastries or desserts. French chefs can qualify for five different certificates, which are like degrees from American colleges. There is a competition every third year, like the Olympics, and the winner may use the letters M.O.F. after his name and (maybe) becomes famous.

祖母的厨房
Grandma's Kitchen

我在空调房里冻得瑟瑟发抖。其实我从来都不习惯公寓楼里旋动的寒冷的气流。我更喜欢打开窗户，去迎接那金黄炙热的太阳，但是公寓监管人却不知为何把整栋楼的窗户都关闭了起来。

拉梅什从学校回到家还要几个小时的时间，我知道他最近一直在忙一个研究项目，每天都要很晚才回家。我冻得全身发抖，看着早上在特产市场采集的蔬菜、香草和调味香料，却不知道晚上做什么菜才好。即使在美国已生活了五年，但我发现我还是在寻找我们在印度的生活，包括天天早上去市场购买食物。

当我仔细打量着卷曲的姜黄、鲜亮的橘子和红芒果的时候——这些都是第一次出现在我的购物篮里的东西。这些东西让我想起我们第一次去美国市场的情景——来美国第一个月时，我们不熟悉这座新城市的街道和地标，难免有些胆怯，所以我和拉梅什都是走到公寓附近的餐馆去吃饭。拉梅什用从学校便利店买的物品调制他的午餐，还开玩笑说“便利”是商店提供的唯一能够满足我们需求的东西。当我们几乎尝遍了附近每家饭店的饭菜后，我许诺说要鼓足勇气去超市购物，这样我们就可以在家品尝到渴望已久的饭菜的味道了。

商店很冷，有时是因为自然的冷风，有时是因为店内开了空调。我很庆幸出门时带了块头巾，我将头巾披在裸露的肩膀上。

起初，我对这么多食品及各种五彩缤纷的颜色感到很震惊。但是接着我却惊讶地发现农产品区被隐藏在了离商店门口最远的地方，好像商店对它们感到难为情一样——这里找不到我们最喜爱的食物，甚至是主食。没有干扁豆或鹰嘴豆，没有番荔枝或石榴。我在过道里走来走去，徘徊在用塑料薄膜包好的肉片和一排排印有“家庭装”字样的盒装食物之间，感到惊叹不已。一时无法专注于盒子上的标签，我转向一位穿着制服的正要去把货架上的姜味汽水瓶扶正的青年。

“打扰一下，请问你们能不能帮我找一下……”我请求道。

他瞥了我一眼，注意到我的纱丽，目光锐利且不加批判。“过道七，右边。”他尖声说道，伴随着意料之外的和蔼可亲的爽朗笑声。

我对他把我如此简单地归类感到很恼怒，但看到两货架的酸辣酱和混合果酱后，我的恼怒缓解大半。在那排货架上，我发现一瓶进口的唐杜里肉酱，这是我在印度时最喜欢的一种肉酱。但是当我曲折但成功地找到排队处，为少量熟悉的几款产品付款时，我观察到超市货架上的商品在天花板荧光灯的照射下褪了色。这些瓶瓶罐罐不再具有异国情调和吸引力。对我来说不管标签多么引人注目，生动的颜色在均质的荧光灯的照射下也会不可避免地变得平淡无奇。

我有时还去超市购物，但是最近拉梅什的一位同事建议我们去市郊的一个新开的印度市场购物，今天早上我就去了。负责管理市场的老太太从一个货摊迅速移动到另一个货摊，强烈建议顾客试吃小块的水果或解释什么调料可以为菜肴锦上添花。她让我想起我的祖母，内心顿时痛苦难挨，我的祖母同样确信——和别人分享食物和智慧会让别人的生命更加美好——每当我需要安慰和陪伴的时候我的脑海里都会回忆起祖母的形象。

我的手指划过米褐色的花岗岩石，这让我想起了祖母厨房里粗糙的木质装潢。孩提时，我相信深色的木头里有着每一道切蔬菜时留下的划痕以及祖母用锋利干净的水果刀切割甘甜水果时留下的污渍。我认为被祖母用研钵和杵捣成粉末的十四种香料，每一种都有自己的粗糙质地和微妙但鲜明的颜色。然后我想起了在美国超市里见到的浅灰色的不相宜的咖喱粉，和我祖母费工夫做出的一点儿都不一样，想到这里，我不禁叹了口气。

我现在并不需要马上就做晚饭，我已经学会了将市场新鲜生产的调料与超市里快速备好的调味酱及肉酱混合，所以就不会把晚餐变成像我祖母与母亲那样要忙碌一天才能做完的工作。即使如此，我还是决定穿着印着学校标志的长袖运动衫去抵制严寒，让自己投身于工作中。

Grandma' s Kitchen

I'm shivering in the air conditioning. I've never gotten used to the swirl of chilled air in the apartment. I'd like to open the window, to welcome in the hot bright yellow sun, but the superintendent has painted all the building's windows shut for some unexplained reason.

Ramesh won't be home from the university for several hours, I know. The project he's working on is keeping him at the lab until later in the evenings these days. Still shivering, I mull the choices for our evening meal, scanning the vegetables, herbs and spices I collected at the specialty food market this morning. Even after five years in the United States, I find I still seek the patterns of our life in India, including my daily morning visits to the market to do the day's food shopping.

As I pore over the curled turmeric roots and the bright orange and red mangoes—both of which appeared in the market's bins today for the first time—I remember the first time I went to an American-style supermarket. Intimidated by the unfamiliar streets and landmarks of our new city, Ramesh and I had spent the first month of our American life eating all our meals at restaurants within walking distance of the flat. Ramesh had concocted his lunches from items purchased at the university's "convenience store"; he joked that convenience was really the only desirable thing the shop offered. Once we had exhausted the menus at each of the nearby restaurants, I promised that I would brave the supermarket so we could both have a taste of the home we'd been aching for.

Naturally—or rather, unnaturally—the store was cold, and I was glad I had decided to bring along my dupatta to shield my otherwise bare shoulders.

At first, the enormous quantity of goods and the wildly varied colors everywhere I looked were impressive. But then I noticed that the produce section—it seemed surprisingly tucked away on the end farthest from the doors, as if the store were somehow ashamed of it—lacked items we considered favorites or even staples: no dried lentils or chickpeas, no cherimoyas or pomegranates. I wandered up and down the aisles, wondering at the slabs of meat sealed within cocoons of plastic, and at the seemingly infinite rows of boxes, each of which somehow housed "dinner for the whole family." Unable after a time to focus on the boxes' labels, I turned to a gangly, uniformed teenager who was pretending to straighten the ginger-ale bottles on the bottom shelf.

"Excuse me, please, I am wondering whether you could help me find..." I began.

He glanced up at me, noting my sari with an eye that felt at once piercing and uncritical. "Aisle 7, on the right." he squeaked, with a wide, unexpectedly amiable grin.

My irritation at having been so easily categorized faded somewhat at discovering two shelves' worth of jars of chutneys and mixes, including one imported tandoori paste that had been one of our favorites back in India. But as I unsteadily but successfully navigated the checkout lines and paid for my few, familiar products, I observed that the supermarket's fluorescent ceiling bulbs effectively bleached out the shelves' contents. The bottles and boxes no longer seemed exotic or glamorous. It seemed to me that no matter how insistently the labels tried to draw attention to the wonders within their containers, the vividness of their colors would inevitably appear flat and lifeless under the homogenizing light.

I still go to the supermarket sometimes, but recently a colleague of Ramesh's recommended that we go to the outskirts of the city to shop at a new Indian market, where I went this morning. The old woman who manages the place moves quickly from stall to stall, urging customers to sample pieces of fruit or explaining how adding one more ingredient will perfect the planned dish. She reminds me, almost painfully, of my grandmother, who was similarly convinced that she could make others' lives better through shared food or wisdom—my grandmother, to whose image I've often come back whenever I've needed consolation or company.

I trace my finger along the beige granite countertop, as if conjuring up the rough wooden surface in my grandmother's kitchen. As a child, I'd believed the dark wood had retained every nick from every vegetable chopped, and every stain from every fruit that had yielded its sticky sweetness to my grandmother's swift, sure knife. I think of the fourteen distinct spices, each with its own grainy texture and subtle but memorable color, that she pounded into dust with her mortar and pestle. Then I recall the grayish, unfriendly curry powder I'd seen in the American supermarket, so unlike the familiar result of my grandmother's efforts. I sigh.

I don't really need to begin to prepare our dinner yet. I've learned to combine the specialty market's fresh produce with the supermarket's "quick prep" sauces and pastes, so making dinner isn't the all-day task it often was for my grandmother and even my mother. Even so, I decide to ward off the cold by shrugging on a sweatshirt embossed with the university's logo, and I set myself to work.

完美的炖牛肉
Roast Done Right

与雕刻维纳斯和画西斯廷教堂一样，烹饪美食也是一种艺术。就算看似平凡的炖牛肉，也可以成为一种杰作。对于一名厨师来说，没有什么比香味四溢的炖牛肉更能让人满足了。

做一道美味的炖肉配蔬菜，需要准备三样东西：最新鲜的食材、慢炖锅，以及好时机。我的朋友艾瑞克在早上五点钟肉店开始派送时就赶到了肉店，这样可以拿到最好的肉，然后去当地的农贸市场。从农贸市场回来，他的帆布购物袋里塞满了成熟的西红柿、新鲜的洋葱和深黄色的土豆。鲜美可口的蔬菜是天然的阳光和农民们悉心照料的结果。

提着买来的东西，艾瑞克走进了厨房。他把牛肉用大蒜和香料泡一会儿，将五颜六色的蔬菜切好。然后把泡好的牛肉放进慢炖锅，再把切好的蔬菜小心翼翼地放在肉的周围。接着把橙色的胡萝卜和大块的土豆片一排排覆盖在肉和蔬菜的上面。最后撒了些切成薄片的洋葱和香草，直到食材把锅装满。和许多厨师一样，艾瑞克有一个秘密配方，就是要在最后加入一些红酒用来调味。

然后，盖上锅盖，打开炖锅。锅内的温度慢慢上升，然后咕嘟咕嘟的沸腾着，菜和肉的汁液慢慢被炖出来。炖肉需要六个小时到八个小时，但在一两个小时之后，厨房里就会有香气飘散。再过几个小时，香浓醇厚的肉味便会充溢整个房间。每隔大半个小时，艾瑞克就会用一个长长的肉类温度计来测量肉的温度，并认真查看其他食材的情况。他不希望把肉煮得太熟了，或者没煮透，而是希望它能“刚刚好”。

他将炖好的肉端出来，把鲜嫩的炖肉“扑通”一声放到我们的盘子里，然后又盖上美艳鲜亮、热气腾腾的蔬菜。很明显，艾瑞克很骄傲能和大家分享他的艺术作品，而他的朋友们也非常乐意享用他的创作。

Roast Done Right

Just like sculpting the Venus de Milo or painting the Sistine Chapel, preparing a delicious meal is an art. Even the seemingly mundane pot roast can be a true masterpiece. Nothing can be more rewarding to a cook than the swirling rush of robust aromas of a roast done right.

Cooking a delicious roast with vegetables requires three things: the freshest ingredients, a slow-cooker, and good timing. My friend Eric goes to the butcher shop just after its 5 a.m. delivery to snatch up the best cuts of meat, then heads to the local farmer's market. He fills his canvas shopping bag with ripe red tomatoes, crisp yellow onions, and thick russet potatoes. The tastiest vegetables are the results of natural sunshine and of a farmer's careful tending.

With supplies in tote, Eric heads to the kitchen. While the beef marinates in garlic and spices, he chops the colorful array of fresh vegetables. Eric meticulously layers the finely cut vegetables around the meat in the slow-cooker's pot, alternating rings of bright orange carrots and chunks of the red potatoes. He sprinkles in sliced onions and herbs until ingredients nearly spill over the top. Like many cooks, Eric has a secret, final ingredient: a splash of red wine for flavor.

At this point, it's time to cram the lid onto the heaping potful of ingredients and turn on the cooker. The temperature inside the pot rises slowly to a lazy, bubbling boil, stewing the savory contents in their natural juices. The roast will take six to eight hours to cook, but after an hour or two, the first spicy scents start wafting through the kitchen. A few hours later, the rich, juicy smell of beef begins to escape. Every half-hour, using a long meat thermometer, Eric reads the temperature of the roast and carefully examines the stewing contents. He doesn't want it overcooked or undercooked, but "just right".

As he lifts the finished roast out of the pot to serve, the tender meat plops juicily onto our plates in generous servings. He tops it off with zesty, steaming vegetables. Eric is obviously proud to share his work of art, and his friends are more than willing to eat it.

【第四章】
NO.4

动物长征

Marching Animals

世界语文・美国语文
International Literature American Literature
2

灵长类动物的饮食习性

The Eating Habits of Related Primates

对于生活在250万年前的人类祖先的饮食习惯，科学家知之甚少。为了解决这个问题，科学家开始研究黑猩猩的捕食行为和饮食习性，希望借此可以找到一些线索，弄清楚生活在史前时期我们的祖先的饮食习惯。

选择黑猩猩作为研究目标的优势是显而易见的。现代人和黑猩猩有非常密切的联系。专家宣称黑猩猩的DNA序列有98.5%和人类一致。如果这一说法属实，人类与黑猩猩的关系要比和其他动物的关系密切得多。

20世纪60年代，珍妮 · 古道尔博士开始在坦桑尼亚研究黑猩猩。在此之前，科学家认为黑猩猩是严格的素食者。古道尔博士首次报道了肉类也是黑猩猩日常饮食的一部分。实际上，古道尔博士还发现黑猩猩是熟练的猎手。一只黑猩猩每年要捕食150多只小动物。黑猩猩喜欢捕食的猎物有红疣猴、野生猪和各种小羚羊，其中红疣猴是黑猩猩最重要的猎物之一。一项著名的研究表明，一组黑猩猩所捕食的动物中，红疣猴占了80%多。

尽管如此，科学家还是认为黑猩猩是以水果作为主食的动物。事实上，肉类只占了黑猩猩日常饮食的3%左右。这比人类每天食用的肉类的数量要少得多。研究还表明黑猩猩的捕食行为大部分发生在干燥季节。8月和9月是最适宜的捕猎季节。在干燥的季节，森林的食物短缺导致黑猩猩体重下降，所以，它们会通过食用肉类补给体能。在最干旱的时候，一只成年黑猩猩平均每天摄入的肉类大约达到了65克。这和现代人在其他食物来源较少的情况下所食用的肉类的数量差不多。黑猩猩的饮食习性与早期狩猎采集者也非常接近。

在灵长类家族中，只有人类和黑猩猩有捕猎行为和经常食肉的习惯。不过，人类和黑猩猩一样，并不是真正的肉食动物。事实上，古人的日常饮食是以植物类为主的。即便是现代人也被认为是杂食性动物，因为他们的饮食包括水果、蔬菜和肉类。

很多人以为食物的选择完全是基于营养成本和益处。虽然黑猩猩的捕猎行为主要是在营养需求的驱使下进行的，但黑猩猩的有些行为却不能完全用营养需求来解释。研究人员认为黑猩猩的捕猎行为可能是为了社会地位。例如，一只雄性的黑猩猩可能为了向其他同类展示自己的能力而捕杀猎物。另外，肉类也可能是黑猩猩用于惩罚竞争者和回报朋友的一个政治工具。不过，另外一项研究表明，那些哺育了更健康和强壮后代的雌性黑猩猩每次能享受到大部分的猎物。这表明食用肉类可能对养育后代有益处。

通过研究黑猩猩的捕猎行为所获取的信息对研究我们祖先的饮食习性会有一定的启发作用。不过，我们仍需开展进一步的研究才能获得更有力的证据以揭示史前人类的饮食习性。

The Eating Habits of Related Primates

Scientists know very little about the eating habits of our ancestors who lived over two and a half million years ago. To solve this problem, scientists have started examining chimpanzees' hunting behavior and diet to find clues about our own prehistoric past.

It is not difficult to determine why studying chimpanzees might be beneficial. Modern humans and chimpanzees are actually very closely related. Experts believe that chimpanzees share about 98.5 percent of our DNA sequence. If this is true, humans are more closely related to chimpanzees than to any other animal species.

In the early 1960s, Dr. Jane Goodall began studying chimpanzees in Tanzania. Before the 1960s, scientists believed that chimpanzees were strict vegetarians. It was Goodall who first reported that meat was a natural part of the chimpanzee diet. In fact, Goodall discovered that chimpanzees are actually very proficient hunters. Individual chimpanzees have been known to hunt and eat more than 150 small animals each year. Among the chimpanzees' favorite prey are the red colobus monkey, feral pig, and various small antelope species. The red colobus monkey is one of the most important animals in the chimpanzees' diet. In one notable study, the red colobus monkey accounted for more than 80 percent of the animals eaten by one group of chimpanzees.

Despite these findings, scientists still maintain that chimpanzees are mostly fruit-eating creatures. In fact, meat composes only about 3 percent of the chimpanzee diet. This is substantially less than the quantity of meat consumed by the average human. Studies show that chimpanzees do most of their hunting in the dry season. August and September appear to be the most popular months for hunting. During the dry season, food shortages in the forest cause the chimpanzees' body weight to drop. Consequently, chimpanzees supplement their diets with meat. During the height of the dry season, the estimated meat intake is about 65 grams per day for adult chimpanzees. This is comparable to the quantity eaten by modern human societies whose members forage when other food sources are scarce. The chimpanzees' eating habits also closely resemble those of the early human hunter-gatherers.

Humans and chimpanzees are the only members of the Great Ape family that hunt and eat meat on a regular basis. However, like chimpanzees, humans are not truly carnivorous creatures. In fact, most ancient humans ate a diet composed mostly of plants, and even modern humans are considered omnivores because they eat fruits, vegetables, and meat.

Most people assume that food choices are based solely on nutritional costs and benefits. Although it is clear that the hunting habits of chimpanzees are guided mostly by nutritional needs, some aspects of the chimpanzees' behavior are not well explained by nutrition alone. Researchers suggest that chimpanzees might hunt for social gain. For instance, a male chimpanzee might try to demonstrate his competence to other male chimpanzees by killing prey. Chimpanzees may also use meat as a political tool to punish rivals and reward friends. However, a study also shows that female chimpanzees that receive large portions of meat after a hunt have healthier and stronger offspring. This indicates that there might be reproductive benefits to eating meat as well.

The information that scientists have been able to gather regarding chimpanzee hunting behavior is shedding some light on the eating habits of our ancestors. Further investigation is needed, however, to provide stronger evidence regarding this aspect of man's prehistoric past.

狼群又回来了
Are Wolves Making a Comeback

天刚一亮，一名猎人在美国怀俄明州西北部一片长满松树的陡坡上悄然爬行。当他在寻找麋鹿的踪迹时，发现在一片刚刚飘过雪花的土地上有一个非同寻常的足迹。这个足迹有人的手掌那么大。他想这很可能是狼留下的足迹。

尽管大家普遍认为狼群可能早在很多年前就从这片土地上消失了，上面那名猎人讲述的故事却也不是子虚乌有。很多报道（大多数由猎人提供）都有狼群嗥叫，狼群踪迹，以及疑似被狼所杀的动物的描述。甚至有人声称曾目睹过一片狼群渐渐消失在漆黑的森林里。很多护林员都说曾在晚上听到过幼狼发出的轻柔的叫声。美国林业局已经证实在过去的10年间有30起有关俄怀明州大提顿国家公园有狼出没的报道。

根据美国林业局工作人员的陈述，在19世纪六七十年代，落基山灰狼遍及怀俄明州大部分地区。然而，很多农场工人和政府采取了一致行动，诱捕和毒杀了很多灰狼，以期达到灭绝这一食肉动物的目的。19世纪和20世纪之交，几乎没有一只灰狼幸存。从此，狼便从怀俄明州消失了。

现在狼已经被列为除美国明尼苏达州之外其他下游48个州的濒危动物。20世纪60年代，狼群从加拿大迁徙到明尼苏达州。除此之外，在蒙大拿州北部，还有大量狼群出没。生物学家相信有关疑似狼群在怀俄明州出现的报道表明一些狼一直在向南移动。

尽管林业局工作人员认为有关狼群出没的报道是诚实可信的，但他们需要证实在大提顿地区有狼群和繁衍后代的对狼的足迹。所以，生物学家已经决定自己寻找这些足迹。他们已经飞往麋鹿和鹿越冬的地方。在那里，他们骑着马，开着机动雪橇，驰骋于各个山头。他们甚至向后仰起脑袋，发出一种低沉的呻吟。希望通过模仿狼的嗥叫，能够与狼进行交流。偶尔，有些狼还真会做出回应，发出几声狼叫。

Are Wolves Making a Comeback

At dawn a hunter crept across a steep, pine-covered slope in northwest Wyoming. He was searching for signs of elk when he noticed an unusual track, broad as a human hand, in the newly fallen snow. He thought it might have been made by a wolf.

Even though wolves supposedly disappeared from the area years ago, the hunter's story was not an usual. Many reports—most of them filed by hunters—have recounted howlings, tracks, and possible wolf kills that is, animals killed by wolves). A few people even claim to have stood face-to-face with wolves before the animals faded into black timber. Many other wolf sightings have no doubt gone unreported. The United States forest Service has verified thirty reports of wolf sightings the past decade in Wyoming's Bridger-Teton National forest.

According to Forest Service officials, the Rocky mountain gray wolf was common throughout most of Wyoming in the 1860s and 1870s. However, ranchers and government "wolfers" made a concerted effort to exterminate the predators by trapping and poisoning them. By the turn of the century, there was scarcely a wolf left in the state.

Wolves are now classified as an endangered species all the lower forty-eight states except Minnesota, into which the animals began migrating from

Canada in 1960s. There is also a sizable population of wolves just north of the Montana border. Biologists believe that the recent flurry of possible wolf sightings in Wyoming may indicate that a few wolves are moving south.

Although Forest Service officials consider the sightings to be honestly reported, they need to confirm the presence of wolf packs and breeding pairs in the Bridger—Teton area. So biologists decided to look for the wolves themselves. They have flown to elk and deer wintering areas, ridden horses and snowmobiles through the mountains, and even thrown back their heads and called out with low, moaning howls in hopes of communicating with the wolves. Occasionally the wolves have answered back.

金斑蝶的漫长迁徙路
The Flight of the Butterfly

我们熟悉的黑脉金斑蝶像许多鸟类一样，会随季节变换而迁徙。每年，一亿多只金斑蝶在华盛顿、俄勒冈州和加利福尼亚州北部度过夏天后，会飞往加利福尼亚州南部或墨西哥北部地区。与此同时，栖息在落基山脉东部的金斑蝶则需要飞行长达三千多千米的路程，从加拿大或美国到墨西哥的山区过冬。金斑蝶更多地是依靠季风的推动而非翅膀的力量，来完成每天96千米的路程。

金斑蝶是如何完成长距离迁徙的，便成为科学家们一直在努力解答的一个问题。这些小小的生物是怎么从几千千米之外找到过冬的地方的？一些大型的迁徙动物如非洲庞大的牛群是从它们的父辈或者群中年长的成员那里学习如何找到迁徙地的。鸟类和海洋动物也是如此，比如燕子、鲑鱼和海龟。但上一代的金斑蝶并不能指引它们的下一代完成迁徙。

一只金斑蝶的寿命一般不超过90天，所以这种蝴蝶需要几代的努力才能完成一次南迁。春天飞往北方过夏天的金斑蝶没有一只可以活到秋天的南迁。所以，从缅因州或威斯康星州到墨西哥的漫长旅程中，它们是如何找到去那里的路的呢？

堪萨斯大学的昆虫生态学家最近提出金斑蝶是通过太阳位置的指引才得以在长途旅程中保持正确方向的观点，但这不可能是全部的答案。另外一种解释是，金斑蝶可能能感觉到地球磁场的磁力线，并以此作为导航信息，完成长途迁徙。还有一种理论认为金斑蝶是通过白昼的长度变化来确定飞行方向的。这么小的一种生物如何找到自己的迁徙地依然是个谜。

25年前，科学家偶然发现了金斑蝶过冬的地方。一位美国昆虫学家在塞拉利昂发现了数百万只北美金斑蝶。现在，美国数百名小学生和大学生像研究鸟类一样，给金斑蝶戴上标签，然后观察它们的行踪。其中一只在弗吉尼亚州被标记的蝴蝶已经安全到达了墨西哥。时至今日，我们依然不确定它是如何找到去墨西哥的路的。

The Flight of the Butterfly

Like many birds, the familiar orange and black monarch butterfly is migratory. Each year more than a hundred million of the insects fly from their summer homes in Washington, Oregon, and northern California to areas in southern California and northern Mexico. Meanwhile, the monarchs on the eastern side of the Rockies fly more than two thousand miles from Canada and the United States to mountain retreats in Mexico. Covering as much as sixty miles a day, the butterflies are propelled more by the seasonal winds than by the power of their wings.

The migration raises a question that scientists are trying to answer. How does this tiny creature find its way to a wintering place several thousand miles away? Larger migratory animals like those of the great herds of Africa learn their routes from their parents or older members of the species. So do birds like the swallow, or sea animals like the salmon or sea turtle. But an older generation of butterflies cannot instruct a younger one.

The life span of a monarch is likely to be less than ninety days, so the butterflies that make their way down south are several generations away from their ancestors that made the same trip. Not one of the insects that flew north in the spring is alive to fly south in the fall. How, then, do they find their way to Mexico from points as far apart as Maine and Wisconsin?

Insect ecologists at the Uiversity of Kansas have recently established that the monarchs use the position of the sun to determine their flight direction on longdistance journeys. But this cannot be the whole story. It may be that the butterfly can sense the force lines of the earth's magnetic field and use this as navigational information. Another theory is the butterflies find directional clues in the changing length of the days. How so small an insect can find its way is still a mystery. We still do not have an explanation.

Twenty-five years ago, scientists accidentally discovered the location of the monarch butterflies' winter home. An American entomologist found millions of the North American insects in the Sierra Chinchua. Now butterflies, like birds, are tagged, watched, and counted by hundreds of American schoolchildren and college students. One insect (tagged in Virginia) arrived safely in Mexico, more than two thousand miles away. Exactly how it found its way there is still uncertain.

【第五章】
NO.5

科海迷途

Mysterious Science

世界语文・美国语文
International Literature American Literature
2

聪明女孩的烦恼
The Trouble with Bright Girls

成功的女人深知，在任何一个男性占主导地位的行业里，我们女性常常发现自己处于明显的劣势。我们的能力经常被低估，才能得不到充分施展，甚至连得到的报酬也过低。研究表明，和我们的男性同事相比，职场女性需要在工作上表现出非常高的水平，才能达到胜任中等水平工作的标准。

但是，根据我的个人经验，头脑聪明和有才华的女性很少会意识到，她们最难克服的障碍之一就是存在于她们内心深处的看法。和男性同事相比，我们在判断自己能力的时候，不仅标准更加严苛，方式也有根本性的不同。弄明白我们这么做的原因是纠正我们所犯的可怕错误的第一步。要做到这一点，我们首先需要退后一步看问题。

如果你曾是个非常聪明的五年级女生，现在又是一名成功的专业人士，那么你在职场出人头地的机会还是很多的。心理学家卡罗尔·德维克在19世纪80年代曾做过一系列研究，观察五年级的聪明男女学生如何处理新的困难复杂的材料。

她发现当那些头脑聪明的女孩遇到特别陌生或者复杂的材料时，她们很快就会选择放弃；智商越高的女孩，越容易早早放弃。事实上，成绩全A的女生面对这些材料时，表现得最为无助。然而，那些聪明的男生却将这些困难的问题视为一种挑战，可以激发自己的潜能，从而跃跃欲试。因此，他们会选择加倍努力去解决问题而不是放弃。

为什么会出现这种现象呢？那些聪明的女孩本该是班级里最自信的学生，是什么让她们信心不足？上五年级的时候，女生通常在各门功课中——包括数学和科学——的表现都比男生好。所以，就能力和过去成功的经历而言，这些男生和女生并没有什么差别。唯一的不同在于这些聪明的男生和女生如何解读困难，具体地说就是那些学习起来很困难的材料对他们来说意味着什么。聪明的女生会更快地怀疑自己的能力，然后失去信心，结果导致学习效率降低。

研究者已经弄清楚导致他们对困难的解读出现差异的原因：通常情况下，这些聪明的女生相信自己的能力是天生的，不可改变的，而聪明的男生则认为可以通过努力和练习不断地开发自己的能力。

男孩和女孩是怎么形成这些不同的观点的呢？这很可能和幼儿时期我们从父母及老师那里得到的反馈信息有关。女孩的自制能力一般发展较早，她们更善于听从指示，通常被表扬为“好孩子”。当我们在学校有好的表现时，老师会表扬我们“真聪明”“真机灵”或“真是个好学生”。这样的表扬暗示了机灵、聪明、好等特质是与生俱来的，你要么有，要么没有。

另一方面，男孩总是惹是生非，很难管教。对于父母和老师来讲，能够让他们安静地坐下来并集中注意力就着实是很大的挑战了。这样一来，男孩得到的反馈多是强调努力（例如，“如果你能集中注意力的话，就能学会这个”或者“如果你更努力一点儿，就能把它做对了”。），这样不同反馈的结果是：当他们学习某种新事物觉得很困难时，女孩会觉得这意味着她们不够“好”或“聪明”，而男孩会认为自己不够努力或者不够全神贯注。

我们女性仍然下意识地固守着这些观念，并将其贯穿一生。正是因为聪明的女孩更倾向于把自己的能力看作天生的和不可改变的，所以当她们长大成人后会更加坚信这种看法——当遇到困难的时候，她们会过早地下结论，认为自己没有在某个领域取得成功的能力，从而很快放弃尝试。

即便将所有对女性不利的外部因素统统移除，如机会不均等，大男子主义的成见，为了平衡工作和家庭生活面临的困难和挑战等，我们仍然不得不面对这样一个事实：正是因为我们对自己的能力所持有的错误观念，使得我们成了自己最大的敌人。

你是否经常发现自己会逃避挑战，为求稳妥，只坚持那些容易达成的目标？是否有一些事情，你很早就下结论认为自己绝不可能精通？你是否认为自己永远也不可能掌握某些技能？如果你能列出一长串诸如此类的问题，那么你很可能就是那些聪明女孩中的一员：你认为自己的能力打一出生就已经定型；你被这样的观点困住，而这样的成见对你人生轨迹的改变远远超出你的想象。

研究表明，不管是什么能力——智力、创造力、自制力、魅力，抑或是运动能力，它们都有很强的可塑性。在学习掌握某种技能的时候，你的经验、个人努力和坚持不懈都将发挥很大作用。所以，如果你是一个头脑聪明的女孩，现在是时候把你对自己能力的错误看法抛之脑后，进而接受自己一直在进步的事实，重拾那丢失已久的自信，去从容应对可能出现的任何挑战。

The Trouble with Bright Girls

Successful women know only too well that in any male-dominated profession, we often find ourselves at a disadvantage. We are routinely underestimated, underutilized and even underpaid. Studies show that women need to perform at extraordinarily high levels, just to appear moderately competent compared to our male coworkers.

But in my experience, smart and talented women rarely realize that one of the toughest hurdles they'll have to overcome lies within. Compared with our male colleagues, we judge our own abilities not only more harshly but fundamentally differently. Understanding why we do it is the first step to righting a terrible wrong. And to do that, we need to take a step back in time.

Chances are good that if you are a successful professional today, you were a pretty bright fifth grade girl. Psychologist Carol Dweck conducted a series of studies in the 1980s, looking at how bright girls and boys in the fifth grade handled new, difficult and confusing material.

She found that bright girls, when given something to learn that was particularly foreign or complex, were quick to give up; the higher the girls' IQ, the more likely they were to throw in the towel. In fact, the straight-A girls showed the most helpless responses. Bright boys, on the other hand, saw the difficult material as a challenge, and found it energizing. They were more likely to redouble their efforts than give up.

Why does this happen? What makes smart girls less confident when they should be the most confident kids in the room? At the 5th-grade level, girls routinely outperform boys in every subject, including math and science. So there were no differences between these boys and girls in ability, nor in past history of success. The only difference was how bright boys and girls interpreted difficulty—what it meant to them when material seemed hard to learn. Bright Girls were much quicker to doubt their ability, to lose confidence and to become less effective learners as a result.

Researchers have uncovered the reason for this difference in how difficulty is interpreted: more often than not, bright girls believe that their abilities are innate and unchangeable, while bright boys believe that they can develop ability through effort and practice.

How do girls and boys develop these different views? Most likely, it has to do with the kinds of feedback we get from parents and teachers as children. Girls, who develop self-control earlier and are better able to follow instructions, are often praised for their "goodness". When we do well in school, we are told that we are "so smart" "so clever" or "such a good student". This kind of praise implies that traits like smartness, cleverness and goodness are qualities you either have or you don't.

Boys, on the other hand, are a handful. Just trying to get boys to sit still and pay attention is a real challenge for any parent or teacher. As a result, boys are given a lot more feedback that emphasizes effort (e.g., "If you would just pay attention you could learn this," "If you would just try a little harder you could get it right.") The result: When learning something new is difficult, girls take it as sign that they aren't "good" and "smart", and boys take it as a sign to pay attention and try harder.

We continue to carry these beliefs, often unconsciously, around with us throughout our lives. And because bright girls are particularly likely to see their abilities as innate and unchangeable, they grow up to be women who are far too hard on themselves—women who will prematurely conclude that they don't have what it takes to succeed in a particular arena, and give up way too soon.

Even if every external disadvantage is removed—every inequality of opportunity, every chauvinistic stereotype, all the challenges we face balancing work and family—we would still have to deal with the fact that through our mistaken beliefs about our abilities, we may be our own worst enemy.

How often have you found yourself avoiding challenges and playing it safe, sticking to goals you knew would be easy for you to reach? Are there things you decided long ago that you could never be good at? Skills you believed you would never possess? If the list is a long one, you were probably one of the bright girls—and your belief that you are stuck being exactly as you are has done more to determine the course of your life than you probably ever imagined.

No matter the ability—whether it's intelligence, creativity, self-control, charm or athleticism—studies show them to be profoundly malleable. When it comes to mastering any skill, your experience, effort and persistence matter a lot. So if you were a bright girl, it's time to toss out your mistaken belief about how ability works, embrace the fact that you can always improve and reclaim the confidence to tackle any challenge that you lost so long ago.

健康的假象 A Picture of Health

美国总统约翰·F.肯尼迪一直留给公众很健康的形象。高大修长的身材配上棕褐色的皮肤让他看起来像运动员一样健硕，这可是很多男人梦寐以求的形象。但事实上，他皮肤的棕褐色或许就是阿狄森氏病的早期症状。虽然天生一块运动员的料，但他童年时期的大部分时间都是在病床上度过的，但他强迫自己看起来与在外面玩耍的同龄人一样健康。

在他两岁的时候，他因为患上猩红热而在医院待了两个月。13岁的时候，他得了结肠炎。1940年，他身患严重的骨质疏松症和下背部脊椎压缩性骨折。1944年，他接受了首次背部手术。1947年，他被诊断患上阿狄森氏病。这是一种罕见的自身免疫失调引发的疾病，表现为体重减轻，肌肉松弛，疲劳乏力，低血压以及肤色变暗。1954年和1955年，他接受了背部手术，但两次手术都以失败告终。从那时起，他一直接受慢性疼痛药物治疗，直到1963年去世。

肯尼迪当选时，他每天要服用10～12片药，包括止痉挛药，肌肉松弛剂，各类胆固醇，止痛药和安眠药。此外，他需要接受背部麻醉治疗，有时一天多达6次。

肯尼迪是如何向美国公众隐瞒如此严重的健康问题的？最好的托词就是他的外表：他看起来非常健康。任何见过他的人，不管亲眼见到还是通过电视，都不会怀疑他的健康问题。另外，他非常善于让自己看上去很健康。他可以让除了医生和近亲之外的所有其他人看不出他正在承受病痛的折磨。最后，他准备好了应对所有有关他健康的问题的答案。比如，他把他的背部问题归咎为年轻时在足球场和战场上所受的伤。

或许有人会提出一个更好的问题：像肯尼迪这样一个疾病缠身的人怎么能够胜任美国总统的工作？答案就是肯尼迪具有常人难以想象的能力和毅力。如果将他的疾病和治疗情况与他在任总统期间所作的决策和采取的行动做一个详细的比较，就不难得出如下结论：无论疾病本身的疼痛还是药物产生的副作用，都丝毫没有影响他履行总统一职。

按照今天的标准，肯尼迪的健康问题已经严重到让他有资格申请美联邦残疾人待遇或退休。但是，他不但活了下来，而且出色地完成了自己的使命。

A Picture of Health

President John F. Kennedy's public image was one of enviable health. Tall and trim, he embodied the tanned, athletic image other men sought. In reality, his "tan" was a symptom of Addison's disease. Although genuinely athletic, he had been bedridden for much of his childhood, forced to watch as healthier children played outside.

Kennedy's ailments began with a two-month hospitalization for scarlet fever at age two. At age thirteen, he developed colitis. By 1940, he had osteoporosis and compression fractures in his lower back, and in 1944 he had his first back surgery. In 1947, Kennedy was officially diagnosed with Addison's disease, a rare auto-immue disorder characterized by weight loss, muscle weakness, fatigue, low blood pressure, and darkening of the skin. He underwent two more unsuccessful back surgeries in 1954 and 1955, and took chronic pain medication from that point until his death in 1963.

By the time Kennedy became president, he was taking ten to twelve pills every day, including anti-spasmodics, muscle relaxants, various steroids, pain medications, and sleeping pills. In addition, he received anesthetic injections in his back up to six times a day.

How did Kennedy hide such significant health problems from the American people? His best alibi was his appearance: He looked healthy. His well-being was clear to anyone who saw him in person or on television. In addition, he was well-practiced at acting healthy, and able to hide his crippling pain from all except his doctors and closest relatives. Finally, he was prepared with answers to any health-related questions; for example, he attributed his back problems to old football and war injuries.

Perhaps a better question would be whether such an ill man was competent to be president. The answer is a testimony to Kennedy's incredible strength and perseverance. A detailed time-line comparison of his illnesses and treatments with his official decisions and actions resulted in the following discovery: Neither his illness nor the drugs seemed to have affected his performance as president.

By today's standards, Kennedy had medical problems severe enough to qualify him for federal disability or retirement. Nevertheless, he not only survived but performed at the highest level.

北极的温暖
Warmth in the Arctic

“我们要去哪里？”“去北极之门——夜半太阳国！我们要去挪威的特罗姆瑟！”一学年结束之际，我本来打算回南加州的家里，在那里做救生员，同时利用空闲时间去冲浪。现在，我的朋友却建议我们去距北极圈只有402千米的地方过夏天。他疯了吗？不过现在回头想想，这真是迄今我做过的最疯狂的决定。

虽然特罗姆瑟的天气不算严热，但也不是特别寒冷。偶尔我会穿件羊毛衫，但很少有穿大衣的时候。虽然我不能像往年一样把自己晒成棕褐色，但是当地人的热情弥补了我这一小小的遗憾。我们遇到的每一个人都非常热心地帮助我们。只要我们扫一眼地图，就会有人主动要求（用近乎完美的英语）为我们指路。

其他小镇的人可能会吹嘘自己从来不睡觉，但是在特罗姆瑟，事实就是如此。本来我还担心没有黑夜的漫长时间会很难挨，结果却并非如此。那个夏天，我没有把时间用来坐在救生员椅子上，无聊地用手指旋转着口哨。实际上，我的时间根本不是用来工作或者坐着。那个夏天，我比任何时候睡得都少，但是从来不觉得疲倦。我不确定这是由于午夜阳光的缘故还是香醇的浓咖啡的功劳。

我们大部分的空闲时间都在徒步旅行。在挪威，徒步旅行非常流行。政府还出台了相关法规，如《户外娱乐法案》，确保任何人在野外地区徒步旅行或者滑雪的权利。该法案还补充道：“如果需求增加，政府还会再指定出一些地区用于户外娱乐。史朵史坦宁山是我们最为钟情的徒步旅行地。我们从特罗姆瑟坐缆车直达山顶。从山顶出发，我们从诸多小路中选择其中一条开始我们的徒步之旅。那里的风景真是让人叹为观止。我拍了很多美丽的照片，有清澈的高山湖泊，茂密的白桦林，深邃的峡湾和神奇的午夜阳光。

现在我已返回家中。我期待能够有机会重返特罗姆瑟。不过，下次我要去看看特罗姆瑟冬天的景观。和享受午夜的阳光的心情一样，我现在急切盼望从史朵史坦宁山顶欣赏神秘壮丽的北极光。那里的景观被誉为世界之最，恰如我要赞誉的生活在那里的人。

Warmth in the Arctic

"We're going where?" "To the gateway to the Arctic—the Land of the Midnight Sun! We're traveling to Tromso, Norway!" As the school year ended, I was looking forward to going home to Southern California, where I planned to lifeguard and use my spare time to surf. Now my friend was proposing that we spend the summer 250 miles north of the Arctic Circle. Was he nuts? As I look back, it was the best crazy decision I ever made.

Although the weather in Tromso wasn't hot, it wasn't particularly cold, either. I occasionally needed a sweater, but seldom a coat. And, though I didn't develop my usual summer tan, the warmth of the people of Tromso more than made up for what the climate did not provide. Everyone we encountered was eager to help us. We had only to glance up from a map to find someone offering (in nearly perfect English) to help us find our way.

That summer, my days weren't spent sitting in a lifeguard chair, throwing a whistle around my finger. Other towns may boast that they never sleep, but for Tromso, it seems to be true. Although I feared that the time would drag, the opposite was true. I know I slept less that summer than I ever have; yet, I didn't feel tired. In fact, my days weren't spent working—or sitting—at all. Whether that was the result of the midnight sun or the potently rich coffee, I'm not sure.

Much of our free time was spent hiking. Hiking is so popular in Norway that the government has passed regulations such as the Friluftsleven (Outdoor Recreation Act) that allows anyone to hike or ski across wilderness areas, adding designated areas as demand increases. One of our favorite places to hike was on Mount Storsteinen, which is accessible from Tromso by cable car. From the top, we would hike one of the many trails. The views were amazing. I took photos of clear mountain lakes, thick birch forests, deep fjords, and the midnight sun.

Now that I'm home, I look forward to returning to Tromso soon. However, next time I am determined to see Tromso's sights in the winter. As much as I enjoyed the midnight sun, I am anxious to see the northern lights from Mount Storsteinen, whose vista has been described as world class—exactly as I would describe the region's inhabitants.

弹球和运气
Pinball and Chance

难道现在大家都不玩弹球游戏了吗？几天前，当我带孩子去游戏场玩游戏的时候，我真的好失望，因为游戏场里五彩缤纷地闪烁着灯光的游戏机没有一台是弹子机。电子游戏机充斥了整个游戏厅。

我想我可以理解为什么电子游戏机会比弹子机更受欢迎。电子游戏屏幕里经常可以看到电影明星、怪兽和英雄的身影。在电子游戏里你可以炸毁一座座城市，逃脱地牢的围困，与各种各样的恶棍进行搏斗。但是弹子机却不一样，弹球游戏几乎都一个样子，没有这么多绚丽的画面，也没有上面所说的各种惊险刺激的情节。有些弹子机会比其他的体型大一些，外观漂亮些，但弹子机的游戏规则从来没有发生过变化：你必须手拿着钢球，玩很长时间才能得到一个高分，赢得一场免费的弹子游戏。

然而，电子游戏的吸引力是表面的，短暂的。当你驾驭着你在游戏里扮演的角色突破各种挑战后，你开始认识到电子游戏机是如何回应你的每一个动作的。你知道哪里有危险，哪里可以找到得力的武器。然而，玩弹子游戏时，却很难预测得如此精确。你从来不知道什么时候弹球会远离两侧弹球台，沿着中间直线往前滚动。然而，如果你运气好的话，你以为已经跑掉的一个球会不可思议地反弹回来。

运气让弹球游戏比电子游戏更有趣。大部分电子游戏都是由电脑高手设计而成，你最大的敌人是可以预测的电脑程序。一旦你掌握了一种游戏规则，挑战便不复存在，这种游戏对你来说便失去了吸引力，于是你势必会寻找新的游戏。熟悉了新的游戏之后，你同样会心生厌恶，觉得无聊。如此循环，不断重复。但是玩弹球游戏，你需要考虑三方面的因素：自己、机器和运气。运气有时会成为你的敌人，而有时却是你的盟友。无论你玩过多少弹子机，玩过多少弹球游戏，每次弹球游戏都会有所不同。正是这种不同使弹球游戏一直具有挑战性，一直具有生命力。

Pinball and Chance

Doesn't anyone play pinball anymore? I was disappointed the other day when I took my kids to a game arcade. Not one of the many colorful machines with flashing lights was a pinball machine. Video games filled the room.

I can understand why video games might seem more attractive than pinball. Video screen are populated by movie stars, monsters, and heroes. You can blow up cities, escape from dungeons, and battle all sorts of villains. Pinball machines, on the other hand, are essentially all the same. Some machines are bigger and fancier than others, but the object of pinball never changes: you have to keep a steel ball in play long enough to rack up a high score and win a free game.

The attractions of video games, however, are superficial and short-lived. As you guide your character through the game's challenges, you come to know exactly how the machine will respond to your every move. You learn where the hazards lurk and special weapons are hidden. Pinball, therefore can't be edicted with such accuracy. You never know when the ball will drain straight down the middle, out of reach of both flippers. Then again, you can sometimes get lucky, and a ball you thought was lost will inexplicably bounce back into play.

It is element of chance that makes pinball more interesting than video games. Most video games are designed so that your main opponent is a predictable computer program. Once you have mastered a game, the challenge is gone, and you must look for a new game to conquer. After you learn the new game, you get bored again. The cycle keeps repeating. But in pinball, you have three factors to consider: you, the machine, and chance, which is sometimes your enemy, sometimes your ally. No matter how many games you play on any pinball machine, each game is different. That's what makes pinball a continual challenge.

当电脑感染了病毒
When a Computer Get Sick

不妨想象下这样一个场景：你坐在电脑显示器前，在电脑屏幕前整理着自己混乱的思绪。明天的任务渐渐变得具体化，以文字的形式呈现在你的眼前。突然，在没有任何警告的情况下，你面前的内容消失得无影无踪了。这是不是一场噩梦？其实并非如此。你的电脑很可能出现了故障，检查结果可能是电脑感染了病毒。

计算机病毒类似于寄宿在人体活细胞里的生物病毒。它是种程序，或一组指令。计算机病毒入侵不是给计算机制造故障，就是造成真正的破坏。上面提到的计算机病毒更多的是给计算机制造故障，而非造成真正的破坏。最终，消失了的文字还会重新出现在电脑屏幕上，然而并不是所有病毒都可以自我治愈。

电脑病毒里面破坏性较强的当属一种叫作“炸弹”的病毒。计算机破坏者幕后操纵这些病毒，并在预定的时间内使其爆炸。炸弹病毒可以永久地破坏电脑里面存储的数据。这对电脑的运行来说，无疑是种致命的打击。

与所有疾病一样，治疗病毒的最好的方法是预防。专家建议一定要尽量避免借用别人的光盘，因为光盘很可能携带一定的病毒。专家还建议我们要经常使用杀毒软件对电脑进行体检。专家还说，最好把电脑里的文档备份。这样一来，一旦发现文档感染病毒，你可以果断地将文档删除，因为你手里至少还有备份。专家还指出，如果电脑连接了互联网和万维网，从中下载，复制了一些程序后，电脑还将面临感染隐藏在这些程序后面的新型病毒的风险。

如果电脑系统感染了病毒，要尽快采取恰当的措施，进行查杀和处理。否则，你可能就得坐在电脑面前度过漫漫长夜了。

When a Computer Get Sick

Imagine sitting in front of a computer monitor, filling the screen with your mind's jumbled thoughts. Tomorrow's assignment is slowly materializing before your eyes. Suddenly, without warning, each of the letters in front of you, tumbles to the bottom of the screen. Is this a bad dream? Not exactly. The computer is probably sick, and the diagnosis may be that the computer has a virus.

Analogous to a biological virus that takes over a living cell, a computer virus is a program, or set of instructions, that invades a computer either to create mischief or do real damage. The type of computer virus mentioned above is more mischievous than harmful. Eventually, the letters reorder themselves on the screen. Not all viruses, however, straighten themselves out.

Among the more serious viruses are those referred to as "bombs". Computer, vandals rig these viruses to go off at a preset time. These bombs can permanently destroy data, and that can be disastrous to the operation of a computer.

As with all diseases, the best cure is prevention. Experts suggest that you avoid borrowing computer disks because they might contain viruses. They advise you to give your systems frequent checkups with antivirus programs. They also say that you should make copies of your computer files, so that if a virus does strike and you must delete your infected files, you will at least have backup copies. Experts also point out that using the Internet and World Wide Web has led to new risks of confection in the form of viruses hidden in programs downloaded, or copied, from these resources.

If there is a virus in your system, you had better hope that it responds to the appropriate treatment and therapy. Otherwise, you could be in for a long night at the computer.

祖父的电视遥控器
Grandpa’s Remote Control

祖父不是一个喜欢技术革新的人。至今他还开着那辆1959年生产的雪佛兰英帕拉轿车（他说他简直无法想象要那些无足轻重的装置有什么用，像自动挡或动力转向等）。当他那台老黑白电视机罢工后，他决定去买一台新彩电。当销售员竭力推荐他买一款有遥控器的彩电时，他坚决不要。他说他腿脚尚好，当他想换台的时候，他完全可以不费力气地从椅子上站起来。

然而，销售员仍不放弃，他向祖父热情地讲解遥控器的各种功能，以期吸引祖父的兴趣。他告诉祖父，只要使用遥控器预先设定好他喜欢看的日常新闻栏目的时间和频道，时间一到，他喜欢看的节目便会播放起来。最终，祖父还是买了那台有遥控器的彩电。并且，这台彩电一直到现在还伴随在祖父的左右。

遥控器的各种功能引起了祖父的极大兴趣。他偷偷地告诉我说，当祖母喊他倒垃圾的时候，他会用遥控器把电视声音调大，这个声音控制功能简直太完美了！另外一方面，他说，遥控器上的静音按钮还可以帮他中断电视剧里插播的广告。

祖父最喜欢遥控器的睡眠功能。这一功能可以在一个预定时间后自动关闭电视。当祖父看着电视节目睡着的时候，就显得特别方便。祖父说当他睡着的时候知道电视已经自动关上了，让他感到由衷地开心和带劲。

祖父不仅使用遥控器预定他喜欢看的新闻节目，他还会用来与他最小的孙子开玩笑。当有孩子来他家做客的时候，他会预先设置一个开机时间。时间到后，只见他用手一指，电视便自动打开了。这让孩子感到异常惊奇。他是这样向毫无疑心的孩子解释的：他手指上有一个内置的遥控器。我想祖父尚未学会使用遥控器的所有功能，但毫无疑问，他会继续发现遥控器的新的创造性的使用方法。

Grandpa' s Remote Control

My grandfather is not known for embracing technological change. He still drives his '59 Chevy Impala. (He says he can't imagine needing frivolous options like automatic transmission or power steering.) So, when he went to buy a new color television because his old black-and-white model had finally quit—and the salesperson tried to talk him into buying a model with a remote control, he resisted. He said that he had two good legs and was perfectly capable of getting out of his chair.

However, the salesperson was persistent and, appealing to Grandpa's TV-viewing habits, described the various functions on the remote. Grandpa could punch in the time and the channel of his favorite daily news program, and the TV would turn on that program at the proper time. In the end, Grandpa did buy the remote, and it has since become something he uses all the time.

Grandpa is intrigued by the various uses for that remote. He has confided in me that the volume control is perfect for turning up the sound whenever Grandma asks him to take out the garbage. On the other hand, he says, the button that mutes the sound lets him cut advertisers off in midsentence.

Grandpa's favorite feature on the remote is the sleep function. This option automatically turns the TV off after a preset amount of time, which is very convenient when he falls asleep while watching a show. Grandpa says that to know his TV is doing what he wants, even when he sleeps, is a source of both pleasure and power for him.

As for the programming function, Grandpa not only uses it for the news but for playing jokes on his youngest grandchildren. Explaining to the unsuspecting child that he has a remote control implanted in his little finger. Grandpa points his finger at the TV and, to the child's amazement, seemingly turns it on. I suppose Grandpa hasn't learned all the possible uses of the remote control, but I don't doubt he will continue to discover new and creative ways of using it.

放射性的新用途
New Application of Radioactivity

近来，放射性一个有趣的应用是用来测定含碳物质的年龄。通过测定含碳物质内部的放射性碳-14的含量，就可以推断其年代。这种碳-14测年的方法，是由美国物理化学家威拉德·弗兰克·利比发明的。使用这种方法可以测定含碳物质的年代，精确到只有200年的误差范围之内。目前，这个方法可以用来测定不超过50，000年的样品。

碳-14具有放射性，是宇宙射线的中子撞击大气圈外层的氮原子而形成的，这个过程缓慢而有规律。碳-14性质不稳定，会迅速氧化成二氧化碳；然后经过大气对流，这些二氧化碳与大气内层中的非放射性二氧化碳充分混在一起，形成稳定的混合物，其中每一万亿个二氧化碳分子里就有一个放射性碳-14。植物从大气中吸收二氧化碳时就吸收了碳-14，动物吃进植物的同时吸收了碳-14。一个植物或者动物死亡后，它体内的碳的放射性含量取决于它身体所吸收的碳-14的总量，这个总量又取决于大气中碳-14的浓度。之后，这些死亡动植物体内的碳-14开始以稳定而均匀的速度衰减，其半衰（减）期为5760年，即每过5760年后，就有一半的碳-14消失，其放射性也减为原来的一半。11，520年（两个半衰期）以后，其放射性只剩下原来的四分之一，所含放射性就可以以此类推算下去。

相应地，只要测定出样品里剩下的放射性碳—14的含量，就可以推断出这个样品已经存在了多少年。能够测定的样品包括木头、肉、木炭、皮肤、动物的角，或动植物的残留，等等。

使用传统碳-14测年法测定样品年代时，取碳含量大约为30克的样品，将其燃烧转化为二氧化碳气体及以炭黑形式存在的碳元素，然后用盖革计数器测定炭黑中碳-14的β射线的放射性，再和没有衰减的碳-14的β射线放射性对比，这样，样品的年代就能被推算出来了。研究人员对这个方法的准确性进行了验证。样品是一棵巨大红杉的心材。红杉的年轮显示它被伐倒时已经有2928岁了，这和碳-14测年法测定的结果非常吻合。此外，对埃及第一王朝陵墓里面木材的测定显示，它已有4900年之久，这个数据也是非常可靠的。

New Application of Radioactivity

One of the most interesting recent applications of radioactivity is the determination of the age of carbonaceous materials by measurement of their carbon−14 radioactivity. This technique of radiocarbon dating, which was developed by an American physical chemist, Willard F. Libby, permits the dating of samples containing carbon with an accuracy of around 200years. At the present time, the method can be applied to materials that are not over about 50,000 years old.

Carbon−14 is being made at a steady rate in the upper atmosphere. Cosmic−ray neutrons transmute nitrogen into carbon−14, which is radioactive. The radiocarbon is oxidized to carbon dioxide, which is thoroughly mixed with the nonradioactive carbon dioxide in the atmosphere, through the action of winds. The steady−state concentration of carbon−14 built up in the atmosphere by cosmic rays is about one atom of radioactive carbon to 10^{12} atoms of ordinary carbon. The carbon dioxide, radioactive and nonradioactive alike, is absorbed by plants, which fix the carbon in their tissure. Animals that eat the plants also similarly fix the carbon, containing a trace of radiocarbon, in their tissues. When a plant or animal dies, the amount of radioactivity of the carbon in its tissues is determined by the amount of radiocarbon present, which corresponds to the concentration in the atmosphere. After 5,760 years (the half-life of carbon 14), however, half of the carbon 14 has undergone decomposition, and the radioactivity of the material is only half as great. After 11,520years (or two halflives) only one quarter of the original radioactivity is left, and so on.

Accordingly, by determining the radioactivity of a sample of carbon from wood, flesh, charcoal, skin, horn, or other plant or animal remains, the number of years that have gone by since the carbon was originally extracted from the atmosphere can be determined.

In applying the method of radiocarbon dating, a sample of material containing about 30 grams of carbon is burned to carbon dioxide, which is then reduced to elementary carbon in the form of lamp black. The beta-ray activity of the elementary carbon is then determined, with the use of Geiger counters, and compared with the beta-ray activity of recent carbon. The age of the sample may then be calculated. The method was checked by measurement of carbon from the heartwood of a giant Sequoia tree, for which the number of tree rings showed that 2,928 years had passed since the heartwood was laid down. This check was satisfactory, as were similar checks with other carbonaceous materials, such as wood in First Dynasty Egyptian tombs 4,900 years old, whose dating was considered to be reliable.

简单又复杂的现代视觉

A Simple but Complex Modern Vision

与沃尔特·格洛佩斯和勒·柯布西耶并称为现代建筑的先驱的路德维格·密斯·凡德罗，对于“现代风格”建筑的确立和发展，起到了不可或缺的作用。凡德罗认为，一座建筑应该能够反映它的年龄，哥特建筑和古典建筑无疑就是这方面的典范。凡德罗——他的朋友和学生们都叫他密斯——发现许多建筑师对待建筑设计的态度是有问题的，最突出的问题体现在对老式建筑风格的依赖上。

与他们不同的是，凡德罗试图通过他的建筑来表达他所感觉到的现代感存在的核心原则。他设计的建筑主要以工业钢材和平板玻璃为材料，也就是说，只有代表20世纪生活气息和工业特征的现代材料。密斯只用一些来自美国和德国工厂的少量材料，他想通过这种方式来避免他在当代建筑中发现的主要问题：没有功能的过度装饰造成极大的空间、材料的浪费。密斯发现，使用钢材和平板玻璃可以更好地实现他从早期俄国结构主义的阅读中学到的“效能”的理念，而且使用这些材料，他可以设计出简单、平面、直线的作品。密斯在自己的建筑作品上倾注了大量的时间和精力，希望能够用这些作品来传达简单的设计美，及其内部自由流畅的结构所能带来的复杂美。

凡德罗的建筑学教育是独特的，有许多人甚至将他描述为自学成才的天才。从1908年到1912年，在老师彼得·贝伦斯的指导下，凡德罗成为德国建筑学领域诸多现代和先锋思想的拥护者。从贝伦斯那里，凡德罗看到了开发一种架构思想的可能性。事实上，在古代和现代的许多哲学概念方面，凡德罗都是一位自学专家。哲学帮助他认识了现代世界的特点，带着对于这些特点的成熟的想法，凡德罗着手开创真正属于20世纪的建筑风格。凡德罗致力于为他的作品创造一个哲学、理论的基础，在建筑学的创造和研究领域，他开创了新的词汇。

为了躲避纳粹的压迫，1937年，凡德罗离开德国，来到了美国。在那里，有两项工作正等着他：一个在怀俄明州，另一个在芝加哥的装甲技术学院。凡德罗被聘为学校的负责人，并为逐步扩建的校园做设计工作（这就是伊利诺斯理工学院的前身，现在这所学校规模依然在不断扩大）。为了向学生教授建筑学新的方法和词汇，凡德罗不知疲倦地工作，取得的成绩却非常有限。学生们起初非常热情，但最终，随着20世纪80年代早期后现代建筑的崛起，凡德罗的影响也大不如前了。

但毫无疑问的是，凡德罗在北美城市留下了难以忽视的痕迹。他的建筑不仅在芝加哥、纽约、多伦多等城市独绝天际，更为世界各地的建筑家留下了新的建筑词汇和一系列建筑材料，让他们用以创造更多生活和工作的空间，他也让建筑成为20世纪最伟大的艺术之一。

A Simple but Complex Modern Vision

Ludwig Mies van der Rohe, typically cited alongside Walter Gropius and Le Corbusier as a pioneer of modern architecture, was integral to the founding and proliferation of the "modern style" in architecture. Van der Rohe felt the design of a building should be reflective of its age, as the Gothic and Classical masterpieces surely were. Van der Rohe, called Mies by friends and students, found many architects' attitudes toward architectural design problematic, particularly these architects' reliance on older, outdated architectural styles.

Van der Rohe, instead, sought to express through his buildings what he felt to be the core tenets of modern existence. The buildings based on van der Rohe's designs were primarily constructed into industrial steel and plate glass—that is, only the materials of modern, twentieth-century life and industry. By using only the bare minimum materials produced from American and German factories, Mies sought to cast off what he found to be one of the main problems which contemporary architecture: that overly decorative and ornamental structures with no "function" were wasteful use of space and material. Through steel and plate glass, van der Rohe felt that he could better practice the idea of "efficiency" that he had pulled from his earlier readings of Russian Constructivism, and using these materials as he did to create simple, planar, rectilinear designs, Mies invested his buildings with a strange intensity that conveyed at once the simplicity of design and the complex beauty of the free-flowing structures inside.

Van der Rohe's architectural education was unique, and many describe the architect as largely self-taught. From 1908 to 1912, under teacher Peter Behrens's guidance, Mies became a proponent of many modern and avant-grade ideas in architecture in Germany. From Behrens, van der Rohe began to see the potential of developing an architecture of ideas, and indeed, he was a "self-taught" expert in many ancient and modern philosophical concepts. Studying philosophy helped him to understand the character of the modern world, and with his maturing ideas of this character, van der Rohe set out to create a style truly of the twentieth century. Because van der Rohe was committed to creating a philosophical, theoretical basis for his works, he helped to create a new vocabulary for the creation and study of architecture.

In order to escape the oppressive Nazi regime, van der Rohe left Germany for the United States in 1937. He had two commissions waiting for him there—one in Wyoming and the other one at the Armour Institute of Technology in Chicago. Mies was originally invited to become head of the school and to contribute designs for the school's growing campus (which, as the Illinois Institute of Technology, continues to grow today). To teach pupils his new method and architectural vocabulary, van der Rohe worked tirelessly as an educator, with only limited success. While many students were initially enthusiastic, Mies van der Rohe's influence was eventually eclipsed by the rise of Postmodern Architecture in the early 1980s.

There can be no doubt, though, that van der Rohe has left a huge mark on the look of the North American city. Not only do his buildings help to create the skylines of Chicago, New York, and Toronto, but van der Rohe also gave architects from all over the world a new vocabulary and set of materials with which to create spaces for living and working, and he helped to make architecture one of the great arts of the twentieth century.

【第六章】
NO.6

繁星集

A Myriad of Stars

世界语文・美国语文
International Literature American Literature
2

节日的苦与乐
Holiday Joy (and Chaos)

为什么节日能带给你孩子般的感觉？我可不是指第一次在洛克菲勒中心看到圣诞树被点亮时的惊奇，我指的是那种“我想自己一个人做”的两岁孩子式的任性，在节日刚开始时你热情高涨，你甚至在劳动节刚结束就已经开始期待过圣诞了，你热情满满地期待着这个节日将带给你的各种快乐。

节日的一个重要组成部分就是逛街买礼物。为了避免临时抱佛脚的慌张，你很早就开始了节日购物行动。九月份，你给苏茜姑妈买了一件完美的礼物。你为自己未雨绸缪的英明之举暗自叫好。十月份，你发现了一件礼物特别适合约翰叔叔（他热衷于收集小型鬼雕像）。今年，你的节日购物肯定是小菜一碟！

现在是十一月份，各大广播电台已经开始播放圣诞颂歌。这听起来真傻——离圣诞节还有六周时间呢！你还有足够的时间为购物单上的每个人买礼物。

你突然发现，感恩节到了。你陆陆续续收到了很多节日邀请卡。当你在日历上圈注节日日期的时候，你发誓这个节日一定要和往年有所不同。你发现在你的日程上有几件交叠事件，但并不放在心上。你已经决定好好享受每个节日。

你淡定地列出一长串亲戚和朋友的名字，并在那些已经为其买好礼物的人的名字旁边做了标记。不会吧？十五个亲戚和十二个朋友中，你一共才买好两份礼物！刹那间，节日变成了噩梦。你开始疯狂打电话，问亲戚和朋友希望收到什么礼物，但是无济于事。

你决定凭一己之力为每个人找到合适的礼物，就向商场出发了。你走了很多家商店，目光在琳琅满目的商品之间穿梭，以期找到最完美的礼物。最后，你放弃了，在一家百货商店购买了二十五份普通的礼品券。这些算不上最有创意的礼物，但总算是让你完成了任务。你拖着沉重的双腿，疲惫不堪地赶回家里，开始烤曲奇。突然，你的儿子问你："你给琼斯小姐买了什么礼物？"你号啕大哭起来：你不仅忘了给儿子的老师买礼物，购物清单上还遗漏了另外七个人。你的儿子小心翼翼地走到你身边，给了你一个温柔的拥抱。你感到些许欣慰。你决定把曲奇的事放在一边，先去睡一小觉。当你关灯的时候，你暗暗发誓明年一定要早早着手准备！

Holiday Joy (and Chaos)

Why do the holidays make you feel like a kid again? I'm not talking about the wide-eyed wonder of seeing the tree at Rockefeller Center illuminated for the first time. No, I mean the tantrum-filled, "I want to do it all" attitude of a two-year-old. You begin the season with enthusiasm. You begin thinking about the Christmas season soon after Labor Day, enthusiastically anticipating the many joys sure to unfold.

A critical part of the holiday is shopping for gifts. Not wanting to be rushed with last-minute purchases, you begin your holiday shopping early. In September, you buy the perfect gift for Aunt Susie. You compliment yourself for thinking ahead. In October, you find just the right gift for Uncle John (who collects ghost figurines). This year, your holiday shopping is going to be a snap!

Now it's November, and the radio stations are playing Christmas carols. How silly—we have six weeks until Christmas! There is still plenty of time to find gifts for everyone on your shopping list.

Suddenly, it's Thanksgiving. The holiday invitations begin to arrive. As you mark the dates on the calendar, you vow that this holiday will be different from those in the past. You notice a few overlapping events, but you're not concerned. You are determined to enjoy every holiday occasion.

You calmly begin writing a list that includes names of family and friends, placing checkmarks next to those whose gifts you've purchased. What's this? You've purchased only two gifts out of fifteen relatives and twelve friends? Suddenly, the holiday season has become a nightmare. You begin making frantic phone calls to obtain wish lists, but to no avail.

You rush from store to store. Your eyes dart among the displays for the perfect gift. Finally, you give up and purchase twenty-five generic gift certificates at a department store. They are not the most inspired gifts, but you're done shopping! You trudge home, exhausted, to begin baking cookies. Immediately, your son asks, "What did you get Miss Jones?" You burst into tears, realizing you forgot not only his teacher but seven other people who somehow didn't make your list. Your son cautiously approaches and gives you a gentle hug. You feel a glimmer of joy return. You decide to skip the cookies and get some sleep. As you turn out the lights, you silently vow to start earlier next year!

卡拉OK之乐
Fun with Karaoke

卡拉OK（歌唱伴奏机）是世界范围内最受欢迎的娱乐形式之一。无论在家里，在酒店，还是在晚会上，卡拉OK已经成为一种常见的娱乐形式，它不仅可以使大家度过一段美好的时光，还能给大家带来美好的心理体验。很多人喜欢在自己家里唱歌，这一点我们完全可以理解。然而，既然我们理解人类喜欢在隐蔽的环境里歌唱，为什么还会有那么多人坚持到卡拉OK厅里，站在一群亲朋好友面前，羞涩地演唱呢？对于这个问题，我们可以给出不同的解释。

认真一想，不难发现卡拉OK之所以这么成功的一个主要原因是其浮华而迷人的环境。卡拉OK提供了一种可以让K歌者感觉与往日不同的机会——K歌时他们感觉自己就是歌星。尽管他们的演唱只能在昏暗的酒吧或繁忙的酒店才能听到，K歌的人却感觉自己像在真正的音乐会场演唱，K歌房里有与音乐厅里一样的麦克风、灯光，还有热烈的掌声。尽管他的嗓音平淡无奇，观众还是会报以热烈的掌声，因为他们知道这只是娱乐而已。并且最后大家都想成为一名摇滚歌星。卡拉OK似乎可以使很多人的明星梦在K歌那一刻成为现实，但是这并不是卡拉OK能够保持经久不衰的魅力的唯一原因。

一个更为明显的原因在于与大家一起歌唱会带来很大的愉悦和乐趣。一般我们会在洗澡时，或在车上听广播时，即兴哼起小曲儿。但在卡拉OK厅，我们可以有机会把自己这种通常极为孤独的体验与大家进行分享。无论嗓音好坏，大家都能体验到与他人一起分享音乐所带来的愉悦。在卡拉OK厅里，他人的演唱同样多半是种私人的事情。

卡拉OK对K歌人的影响可能也是其广受欢迎的一个原因：它可以使平时比较腼腆的人摆脱害羞的外壳。卡拉OK厅里，他们克服舞台恐惧，建立自信，战胜自我。K歌的人可能会在第一次登台K歌时紧张，但只要下面的观众给予一定的掌声，他肯定会倍受鼓舞和激励。

不管是出于何种原因，卡拉OK变得越来越受欢迎。去年一年，卡拉OK在日本创收70多亿美元。不少人认为卡拉OK只是一时流行，很快就会过时，但只要它能够给大家带来愉悦和美好的心理体验，它就不会消失。

Fun with Karaoke

Karaoke is one of the most popular forms of entertainment in the world. What defies understanding, though, is why so many ordinary people insist on getting up on age in public, humiliating themselves in front of both their friends and peers. Whether practiced at home, in a restaurant, or at a party, karaoke is a form of entertainment that having provided people with a great time and a positive feeling. It's understandable that people would enjoy singing in the privacy of their homes. There are many different ways to respond to this question.

Look more closely, and you'll see a main reason for karaoke's success is its glitz and glamour. Karaoke provides people with a moment when they are more than just everyday folks—they are stars. Even though their performances may be heard only in dimly lit bars or busy restaurants, karaoke singers are still performing as if in a true concert with such concert–hall staples as microphones, lights, and applause. Even though the singers' voices are not spectacular, the audience knows that it's all for fun and responds anyway. And in the end, everyone would like to be a rock star. Karaoke is as close as many people will get to fame and stardom, but this not the only reason for its enduring popularity.

There is another more obvious reason why karaoke is so popular and singing in public is such fun. The average person allows his or her singing to be heard only in the shower or in the car as the radio plays. Karaoke, by contrast, allows the average person the opportunity to share that ordinarily solitary experience with other people. Regardless of how good or bad their voices are, people can experience the sheer joy of music shared with others, whose singing is mostly a private affair as well, through karaoke.

The effect karaoke has on people may also provide an explanation for its popularity: it helps bring people who are ordinarily shy out of their shells. Karaoke helps them overcome stage fright, build their self-confidence, and conquer their fears. The singers may feel nervous or silly when they first take the stage, but when the audience breaks out into applause, the singers are sure to feel rewarded.

Whatever the reason, karaoke continues to grow in popularity. Last year, karaoke made no less than $7 billion in profit in Japan. Many dismiss it as a fad, but as long as karaoke fun and leaves people feeling good, it will not disappear.

我们的文学杂志社
A Literary Magazine

如果你想成为“游乐园”杂志社的一名员工，你必须有着自我督促的意愿。“游乐园”杂志一年三期。我们的编辑一年到头都不得清闲，每天都有做不完的工作要做。

“游乐园”是各种文学体裁的混合体，包括诗歌、短片小说、散文等文学作品。伴随着一年一度的募集资金和优惠促销活动，我们杂志社在每年7月开始一年的出版工作。我们办公室堆满了订阅单和各种各样的宣传图册。我们必须对这些宣传图册进行分类、捆绑，然后亲自提到邮局去邮寄。

8月，我们把邀请信寄给我们喜欢的作者，邀请他们为我们杂志社投稿。同时，我们也会收到很多其他作者主动投来的稿件。9月和10月期间，我们审阅和评估上百篇各种体裁的稿件。

有些稿件是用铅笔书写，潦草难辨；而有些稿件则是专门打印出来，清晰易读。有些人写信来赞美作者的写作天赋；有些则是谦虚客套的歉意表述。但无论是什么内容，我们只会依据作品的优劣做出刊登与否的决定。我们编辑已经达成一致，每一期杂志必须要保证质量，且要反映出美国文化的多样性特点。基于这种标准，很多文章都存在一定讨论的空间，编辑们必须时刻做好准备，与其他持相左观点的同事进行讨论，为自己的观点勇敢地辩护。

11月份，我们必须从大量的稿件中选出足够三期刊登的文章。一旦我们发现适合作为封面的图片，编辑生产的工作也就开始了。我们精心布置每期杂志的每一页内容，从头到尾，从不含糊。

新年刚过，第一期杂志的内容就会邮寄到排版公司。这一期杂志刚刚搞定，我们就要开始准备下一期的内容。这样一来，一旦第一期印刷的样刊寄回来进行校对，我们就会把第二期的内容邮寄给排版公司。当所有校对工作都完成后，我们把三期内容一并寄给印刷公司。印刷公司负责印刷，装订，然后直接送到我们杂志社。我们的办公室再次被装得满满的，到处是印刷成册的杂志。紧接着，我们会把这些杂志寄给订阅者、评论家和投稿人。直至仲夏时节，我们才能完成一年的任务。不过，新一年的出版发行任务已经接踵而至。

A Literary Magazine

If you want to work for Fairground, you have to be willing to push yourself. The editors of our triannual literary magazine are kept busy all year with a wide variety of tasks.

Our year begins in July, with fund–raising and promotion for the magazine, which presents a mixture of poetry, short stories, and essays. Our office fills up with subscription forms and fliers that we must sort, bundle, and tote to the post office to be mailed.

In August, we send letters to our favorite authors, inviting them to send manuscripts. Meanwhile, we're receiving unsolicited submissions from other writers. During September and October, we read and evaluate hundreds of manuscripts.

Some offerings are scrawled in pencil; others are expertly typed. Some arrive with letters proclaiming the writer's genius; others come with apologies for taking up our time. We base our decisions only on the work itself. The editors agree that every issue has to be good and has to reflect the cultural diversity of the United States. Within that policy there's plenty of room for discussion, and editors have to be ready to argue spiritedly for their choices.

By November, we have selected enough material to fill three issues.

Once we've found artwork suitable for the covers, editorial production begins. We plan the contents of the year's issues, page by page.

Just after New Year's Day, the first issue is mailed to a typesetter. While that issue is being set, we complete the next one's layout. Thus as soon as an issue comes back from the typesetter for proofreading, the next can go in for typesetting. After the proofreading is done, each issue is sent to a printer, who prints it, binds it, and delivers it to our door. Our office fills up again with the printed copies, ready to be mailed to subseribers, reviewers, and contributors. Finally, in midsummer, we ship out our third and final issue—just in time to begin another publishing year.

粗鄙的文明
Crude Sophistication

在现代人看来，住在斯堪的纳维亚半岛（现在的挪威、瑞典和丹麦）的维京人过的是一种粗鄙的生活。但是，他们在很多方面比同时代的其他人先进得多。虽然我们都认为是克里斯托弗 · 哥伦布于1942年第一个发现美洲大陆的，但维京探险家似乎比哥伦布更早到达美洲大陆。实际从某种程度上讲，维京人比晚他们几个世纪的欧洲人更熟悉海洋上的生活。

维京人是最早的海上商人之一，他们为海上交易专门制造了木质的商船。他们从斯堪的纳维亚半岛起航，经由直布罗陀海峡到达地中海东部。这些勇敢的探险家还横渡了大西洋，最后选择在冰岛和格陵兰岛定居。维京人从冰岛和格陵兰岛出发，经过较短的航程来到了北美大陆。目前已经在加拿大的纽芬兰北部找到了维京人到达北美大陆的考古证据。不管维京人是否先到达北美大陆，单单是他们在9世纪至12世纪所完成的这些漫长的航程，就足够让人惊叹不已。

维京人很擅长造船和航海。他们那些古老的码头上停泊着小型的河船，远洋的货船，甚至有战船。这些战船是他们用来袭击他们的基督教邻居的。维京商人将商船驶入波罗的海，在那里交易得到毛皮和琥珀。他们和阿拉伯商人在俄罗斯碰头，用商品交换他们的丝绸和香料。

维京人拥有很多复杂的工艺技术，是技艺高超的工匠。比如，他们的钢剑和斧刃往往都镶嵌着精美的银制图案。类似的制作工艺还被皮革工人用于制造鞋、挽具和马鞍。维京妇女同样掌握不少技能，包括制作奶油和奶酪，以及酿造麦芽酒等。她们还能够将精美的几何图案编进她们彩色的织物里。

维京人落后于同时期其他人的一个方面是阅读和书写。能读会写的维京人不多，所以那些能够识文断字的少数维京人倍受尊敬。他们将维京人的英勇事迹都刻在大石头上。他们所使用的字符被现代人称作如尼文字，由16个不同的符号组成。因为绝大多数维京人看不懂这些文字，所以他们认为这些如尼文字有神奇的力量，可以用来施展魔法。关于维京人的历史和信仰留下来的文字记录很少，我们所知道的一些关于维京人的信息都来自考古发现和其他见过他们的人留下来的文字记录，如他们的基督教邻居（和俘虏），以及和他们有过交易往来的阿拉伯人。

Crude Sophistication

The Vikings of Scandinavia (what is now Norway, Sweden, and Denmark) led what would today be considered a crude existence. In many ways, however, although Christopher Columbus is credited with "discovering" America in 1492, Viking explorers appear to have reached North America much earlier. In fact, to a great extent, Vikings seemed more at home on the ocean than did other European cultures even centuries later.

The Vikings were among the first international seafaring traders with purpose-built, wooden trading ships. Vikings sailed from Scandinavia through the Straits of Gibraltar to the eastern Mediterranean. These intrepid explorers also crossed the Atlantic Ocean, settling in Iceland and Greenland. From there, the Vikings crossed a much shorter distance to the North American continent, where archaeological evidence of their landing has been found in what is now northern Newfoundland, Canada. Regardless of whether Vikings arrived first, their distant travel during the ninth to twelfth centuries is quite remarkable.

Vikings were skillful boatbuilders and sailors. Their ancient marinas included small river boats, ocean-going cargo ships, and even warships used to raid their Christian neighbors. Viking traders sailed into the Baltic sea, obtaining furs and amber. In Russia, they met up and traded goods with Arab traders carrying silks and spices.

Vikings possessed many complicated skills and were fine craftsmen. For example, their steel sword and ax blades were often inlaid with intricate designs in silver. Similar craftsmanship was used by leather workers on shoes, harnesses, and saddlery. Viking women also possessed diverse skills, including making butter, cheese, and ale, and often weaving intricate geometric designs into their multi–colored fabrics.

One way in which the Vikings were behind their contemporaries was in reading and writing. Few Vikings could read or write, so those who could were considered valuable. Records of brave deeds were etched on large standing stones called runes. These runes were made up of sixteen different symbols. Because so few Vikings could read, they believed that runes were magical and could be used to cast spells. Because they wrote down very little of their history or beliefs, most of what is known of the Vikings today is the result of archaeologists' discoveries and written records of people who met them, such as their Christian neighbors (and victims) and the Arabs with whom they traded.

铃木音乐教学法

The Suzuki Method

20世纪30年代初，铃木镇博士正在日本皇家音乐学院教授小提琴，一位父亲把自己4岁的儿子带了过来，请求师从铃木镇学习小提琴。尽管铃木镇先生之前从来没有教过这么小的学生，他还是勉强接受了第一个幼龄小提琴学生。

当铃木镇先生正在揣摩什么训练方式合适这位学龄前学生时，他开始思考小孩是如何用极其复杂的方式学习语言的问题。他觉得这种看似奇迹的学习过程可能为所有学习活动提供有价值的认识，包括学习弹奏一种乐器，比如小提琴。

铃木镇先生已经意识到沉浸式学习法在孩子语言发展的过程中起着非常关键的作用。新生儿每天都沉浸在良好的语言学习环境中。当婴儿第一次牙牙学语，试图发出一种声音的时候，孩子的父母异常兴奋，并开始鼓励和引导孩子日后发出更为精确，更为复杂的声音。老师为学生提供深入的语言解析，孩子会因他们提高了交流技能而受到老师的表扬。基于此，铃木镇先生发明了一种独特的小提琴教学法——铃木镇音乐教学法。铃木镇音乐教学法目前已经成为一种备受世人瞩目的知名音乐教育理论。

铃木镇教学法是指学生充分沉浸在音乐中。学生及学生的家人每天都要听日后将要学习的那种乐器所要弹奏的曲子。当学生弹奏那首曲子的时间，他已经对那首曲子非常熟悉。孩子早期学习音乐的激情和在音乐学习方面取得的成绩密不可分。音乐课堂为孩子提供专业知识训练，小组演奏和音乐会为孩子提供音乐共享的机会。

几十年来，铃木镇先生一直在鼓励学生和老师都进行终身学习。他在世界范围内倡导这样一种观点：每一个孩子都有着成为一名音乐天才和感受成功带来的喜悦的潜质。每一个受到他的启发或受到他的教育影响而演奏的音乐的人，内心都会倍感充实。

The Suzuki Method

In the early 1930s, while Dr. Shinichi Suzuki was teaching violin at the Imperial Conservatory in Japan, a father brought in his four-year-old son for lessons. Although Suzuki had never taught anyone so young, he reluctantly agreed to accept the tiny violin student.

As he pondered what training might work for this preschooler, Suzuki began to think about how young children learn to use language in very sophisticated ways. He suspected that this miraculous-seeming process might offer valuable insights into how all learning occurs, including learning to play a musical instrument.

Suzuki already understood that immersion is a key to a child's language development. Newborns are immersed in language. Babies' first attempts at speech generate excited responses from adults who encourage and guide the children toward more precise and complex speech. Teachers provide in-depth language understanding, and children are rewarded for improving their communication skills. Based on these realizations, Suzuki developed a unique approach to violin studies. His program has since grown into an internationally acclaimed philosophy of music education.

In the Suzuki method, students are immersed in music. Each day students and their families listen to recorded music that the students later learn on an instrument. When the time comes to play a composition, the student already feels intimately familiar with it. The child's early musical accomplishments are greeted with enthusiasm. Lessons provide expert assistance; group sessions and concerts reward students with opportunities to share music.

For many decades, Suzuki encouraged students and teachers alike to strive toward lifelong learning. Worldwide, he promoted the idea that every child possesses the potential to develop musical talent and to experience the joys of achievement. All who hear the beautiful music that his teaching inspired are enriched.

环城高速公路：华盛顿高速公路

The Beltway: Washington's Expressway

如果你像我一样最近来我们的首都华盛顿参观，你很可能会计划参观几大著名的景点，包括华盛顿纪念碑和林肯纪念堂。这些标志性的建筑旨在激起人们的爱国情操和对自己祖国倍感骄傲和自豪之情。然而，我此行印象最为深刻的却是华盛顿环城高速公路。这一高速公路看似已经成为我们疯狂的现代生活的一座纪念碑。

这条环城高速公路对普通高速公路，正如太空穿梭机对普通飞机。它有十条车道那么宽，比我在印第安纳波利斯和辛辛那提行驶过的旁通环路开阔多了。可能是由于它延伸至两个人口密集的州（弗吉尼亚州和马里兰州）且与很多小型公路纵横交错，这条环城高速公路相当繁忙。不仅如此，行驶在这条环城高速公路上的车辆行驶速度也相当快：每天穿梭在上班和回家路上的数千个住在华盛顿的人，有时会忽视路边标示的限制速度。这条环城高速公路的一大可取之处是行驶在这条公路上，你不用担心有迷路的可能。如果你一直驱车前进，行驶一段时间之后，你会发现你环城绕了一圈，并且又回到了起始的位置。

起初，我计划避免选择这条道路。当时我正与朋友一起，在他们弗吉尼亚郊区的家里做客。我请求他们给我提供另外一条风景更为独特的行驶路线。但是，通过他们那种困惑的表情，我意识到他们早已经屈服于华盛顿环城高速公路了。所以，我不得不极不情愿地摸索着在这条公路上行驶。当我驱车驶近这条高速公路的时候，我感到它就像一种不可预测的大自然的力量，需要小心谨慎地监视和控制。它是不是已经堵上了？可以自由通行吗？完全堵死了吗？路途遇到施工设备区怎么办？车载收音机为我提供最新的路况信息。就像一些正在度假的游客时刻关注天气状况一样，我想时刻了解这条高速公路的交通情况。

我不确定通过这次华盛顿之旅学到了多少美国的历史，因为我所有的精力都集中在了阅读道路标志上，但是我驾车并入高速道路的能力有了极大的提高！

The Beltway: Washington' s Expressway

If you visit our nation's capital, as I did recently, you will probably plan trips to several of the famous memorials there, including the Washington Monument and the Lincoln Memorial. These celebrated landmarks were designed to inspire feelings of patriotism and pride. Nevertheless, the structure remember most vividly from my trip was an expressway called the Washington Beltway, which seems to be a memorial to the frenzy of modern life.

This expressway resembles an ordinary highway about as much as a space shuttle resembles an airplane. At ten lanes wide, it is much larger than the bypass loops I have driven around Indianapolis and Cincinnati. The beltway is also far busier, perhaps because it extends through two populous states—Virginia and Maryland—and intersects with many lesser highways. It's also fast: the thousands of Washingtonians who dash from home to work and back sometimes ignore the posted speed limit. The one redeeming feature of the beltway is at it's impossible to get lost on it. If you keep driving long enough, you will eventually circle the city and return to the point where you began.

Initially, I planned to avoid driving on the beltway. I was staying with friends in their suburban Virginia home, and I asked them for help with alternate, more scenic routes. But by their puzzled looks, I realized they had surrendered to the beltway long ago. So, unhappily, I learned to navigate this expressway. I approached it as if it were an unpredictable natural force that required careful monitoring. Was it congested? Moving freely? Blocked completely? What about construction zones? The radio provided me with frequent updates. Just as some people on vacation like to keep a close watch on the weather. I wanted to keep track of beltway conditions.

I'm not sure how much American history I learned on my trip, as my powers of concentration were taxed merely reading road signs. However, my ability to merge in traffic improved immensely!

旧法新用 Modern Uses for Old Ways

乍一眼，简·普莱曾特的试验田乱得一塌糊涂。园地崎岖不平，遍地是高突的土丘，地面上铺满了一层厚厚的枯枝败叶，豆角从玉米秆上爬下来，南瓜秧到处蔓延。但这种表面上的混乱正是科学研究的主题。普莱曾特女士的试验田效仿的是北美易洛魁人和其他印第安人的庄稼地。从这块田地上采集的数据很可能为使用旧方法提高现代农业的理论提供证据支持。

简·普莱曾特本人是易洛魁人，她是康奈尔大学的农业学家。她对现代农业的一些做法提出了质疑，她的观点已被其他农业学家所接受。很多农民和农业学家都认为，现代农业由于过度开垦土地和过度依赖除草剂和杀虫剂其所带来的农作物的高产丰收，伴随而来还有一些隐性成本。土地侵蚀和环境污染已经把我们的食物供应和身体健康置于危险的境地。

易洛魁人的种植方法包括：玉米之间保持0.9米的距离；在新种植的玉米秆旁高堆土层，以便于排水和土壤的保暖；土丘上种植豆角；土丘间种植南瓜。

玉米、豆角和南瓜俗称易洛魁“三姐妹”，易洛魁人往往把它们作为一个组合，套种在一块田地上。玉米秆支撑豆角秧，豆角的根有着固氮作用，所以可以提升土壤的质量；宽大的南瓜叶又可以遏制地上的杂草生长。收获之后，植被的秸秆留下腐烂，再次增加土层的营养，并起到减少潜在土壤侵蚀风险的作用。普莱曾特女士发现她的试验田收成并不亚于那些高科技，单一耕种的农田。她的实验帮助农民在种植保护土壤的覆盖作物时做出更好的决定。

易洛魁“三姐妹”耕种法已经被广为实践了长达4个世纪之久，也许这便是对这种耕种方法最好的支持。普莱曾特曾写过这样一句话：作物高产和土壤保护之间有种平衡。

Modern Uses for Old Ways

At first glance, Jane Mt. Pleasant's garden plots look a total mess. The ground is bumpy with mounds and covered with old leaves. Beans hang on the cornstalks, and squash vines sprawl everywhere. But this apparent chaos is the subject of scientific research. Mt. Pleasant's gardens are modeled on those grown by the Iroquois and other Native peoples. The data the gardens are yielding may provide evidence to support the use of old methods to improve modern agriculture.

A Cornell University agronomist and an Iroquois herself, Jane Mt. Pleasant questions some of modern agriculture's practices, and her concern is shared by others. Many farmers and agronomists believe that the recent boom in crop production—fueled by the intensive use of farmland and increased dependence on herbicides and pesticides has come with hidden costs. Soil erosion and pollution have put our food supply and our health at risk.

The Iroquois method begins with corn being planted three-foot intervals. Later, soil is mounded around the young stalks because of enhancing drainage and warming the soil. Beans are then planted on the mounds, squash is planted between the mounds.

Corn, beans, and squash—the Iroquois "three sisters"—work as a team.

The corn stalks support the bean vines, the nitrogen-fixing roots of the beans enrich the soil, and the squashes' broad leaves stifle the weeds. After the harvest, the remains of the plants are left to rot, further enriching the soil and reducing the potential for erosion. Mt. Pleasant has found that total crop production in her experimental plots rivals that of high tech, single-crop farming. Her research is helping farmers make better decisions about planting soil-protecting cover crops.

Perhaps the best endorsement of the Iroquois "three-sisters" system is that it has worked for over four centuries. Mt. Pleasant notes, "It is a balance between production and soil protection."

寻求冒险
Thrill Seeker Wanted

正如那位平时沉稳持重，业余时间喜欢大胆冒险的大学教师印第安纳·琼斯一样，我的爸爸在白天是一位商人，到了晚上就成了一位寻求刺激的冒险家。他的热情影响了我，我也很幸运地在许多探险活动中都成为他的伙伴。刚开始，我们一起征服了美国速度最快、弯度最大的过山车，之后，我们穿越了大峡谷，又在雄伟幽暗的科罗拉多河进行漂流游览。这次漂流活动开启了我们在全世界寻求冒险的旅程。

世界上的每一个角落，都有惊险和刺激在等待着我们。高空跳伞本身就是一种非常有趣的活动，我们从惊险的瑞士阿尔卑斯山乘坐直升飞机，然后纵身一跃，乘伞跳下，这种刺激终生难忘。我们也曾经在潮湿阴森的秘鲁山洞探险，从世界最高平台南非的克朗桥上蹦极。我们也曾到新西兰体验滚波球冒险活动，这是一种奇怪的运动，参与者先钻进一个巨大的充气气球，然后滚下陡峭的、长满植被的山丘。最近，在瑞士的因特拉肯，我们尝试了“峡谷漂流”，这是最让我们兴奋的一次冒险。

所有喜欢挑战冒险刺激的人，都应该尝试下峡谷漂流。冒险开始，我们顺着27米的绳索爬下峡谷壁，进入一条冰冷的、水流湍急的河流，要是没有防寒衣的话，我们一定会被冻成冰棍！我们勇敢地穿过刺骨的河流，朝我们的目的地河口走去。到了河口，我们就可以看到因特拉肯盆地的全景了，这也便成了对我们此行的奖励。

我们不得不在湍急的河流和光滑的峡谷壁上航行，所以我们就像两栖动物一样，在陆地和河流之间移动。这一刻，我们在光滑的岩石上滑行，下一刻，我们跳下瀑布，在水底隧道里漂游。我们攀上绳梯，滑下飞锁，跳进清澈的河流，然后又攀上绳梯，滑下飞锁，跳入山水之间。如此循环，刺激不断。当然，每次冒险都存在由于错误计算而产生的危险，而这些危险又会让我们产生继续冒险的冲动。峡谷漂流，不管在岩石的表面还是寒冷的河水中，都惊喜不断，刺激连连。

不过，峡谷漂流只能在某些特定的地方进行，而刺激和冒险却是无处不在的。我们在美国开始的那段冒险就是这样。我们继续寻找大的刺激，但在这样做的同时，我们也学会了从日常生活中去寻找一些小的冒险。毕竟，我们不能每天都去峡谷漂流，小的冒险对于我们这些寻求刺激的人来说，总是聊胜于无的。

Thrill Seeker Wanted

Like Indiana Jones, the staid college professor who undertakes daring adventures in his spare time, my father is a businessman by day and a thrill-seeking adrenaline fanatic by night. His enthusiasm rubbed off on me, and I have been lucky to be his sidekick on many an adventure. We started out small by conquering America's fastest, most twisted rollercoasters. After that, a whitewater rafting excursion through the Grand Canyon on the majestic, if murky, Colorado River jumpstarted our search for other extreme thrills across the globe.

Spectacular thrills awaited us at every corner of the world. A remarkable activity in its own right, skydiving was especially momentous performed from a helicopter over the breathtaking Swiss Alps. We have gone spelunking in damp and ominous Peruvian caves. We have bungee jumped from the world's highest platform, Bloukrans Bridge in South Africa. We have traveled to New Zealand for Zorb, a strange activity in which participants enter a giant, inflatable ball and roll down steep, grassy hills. Most recently, in Interlaken, Switzerland, we attempted "canyoning," which was our most exhilarating adventure yet!

Anyone who loves a challenging thrill should try canyoning. Our adventure began with a 90-foot rappel down a canyon wall into a rushing, ice-cold river, and without wetsuits we surely would have become popsicles! Intrepidly, we traversed the bone-chilling water toward the mouth of the river, our final destination, where the reward for the journey would be a panoramic view of the Iush Interlaken basin.

We had to navigate both the flowing river and the canyon walls, so we became amphibious, moving seamlessly between land and water. We slid over slick rocks at one moment, leapt from waterfalls and swam through underwater tunnels the next. Back and forth we alternated, scaling rope ladders before zooming down zip lines back into the fresh mountain water. Certainly, danger from miscalculations was lurking in each of these activities, but that very danger provided the rush. Canyoning was indeed one thrill after another, both on rocky surfaces and in the chilly water.

While canyoning is possible only in certain locales, thrills and adventure can be found anywhere. Our humble beginnings in the U.S. showed us just that. We continue to seek the big thrills, but in doing so, we have learned to seek lesser forms of excitement in daily life as well. After all, we can't go canyoning everyday, and small thrills are better than none for us thrill seekers.

在农场长大
Growing Up on a Farm

早在上中学的时候，我曾经和妈妈在她的农场生活了两年。每当人们听说我在农场生活过，他们头脑中马上就会出现一幅有奶牛、拖拉机、干草和工装裤的画面，但这些和事实都相差太远了。

首先要说的是，我并不是在大家所想象的那种农场，我不喂猪也不喂牛，不种玉米也不种麦子，我只是帮妈妈饲养美洲驼。

奇怪的是，我们这种历史悠久、世代相传的农场竟然会饲养这种不同寻常的家畜。我们家族种植农作物、果树和饲养传统家畜已经几十年了。五十年前，我的曾祖父决定买一头美洲驼，想必他一定是认识到了美洲驼的毛比羊毛更值钱。后来，骆驼毛生意发展得很成功，曾祖父也干脆把我们的家族企业转变成了一个成熟的美洲驼养殖农场。

在我住进农场之前，对农村生活也抱有着天真的幻想。还有什么比饲养一些动物更容易的吗？但是，等我在新家安顿下来之后，我发现农村生活比我预期的复杂得多。比如说捡粪这项工作，在电视上看别人做也没觉得那么糟糕，但我不得不在天亮前起来，干完活之后还要赶公交车去上学。

农村的学校和我预想中的也大不相同。我所在的那所学校一共有二十名学生：这是从一年级到十二年级的学生总数，而我是我们年级唯一的学生。我们只有一位老师，偶尔他会就某一个话题进行讲解，但大部分时间，我都是抱着课本自学。

我并不是说在农场的生活是段糟糕的经历。事实上，通过这段经历我对自己有了更多的了解，比如说，我不是一个习惯早起的人。我也了解了很多美洲鸵的习性，比如它们不高兴的时候就会吐口水。最重要的是，在这段时间里，我可以经常和妈妈在一起，为此我感到非常庆幸。虽然我不觉得自己将来会从事农业工作，但依然期待有机会可以再回到农场住一段时间。

Growing Up on a Farm

Back in middle school, I went to live with my mother for two years on her farm. Whenever people hear that I lived on a farm, they immediately conjure up an image of dairy cows, tractors, hay, and overalls. Nothing could be further from the truth.

To start, I wasn't on the kind of farm everyone imagines. I didn't feed cows or pigs; I didn't grow corn or wheat. I helped my mother breed llamas.

It is odd that such non-traditional livestock should be raised on a long-established farm such as ours, which has been in the family for generations. Our family did indeed grow field crops, harvest orchards, and raise traditional live stock for many decades. Then, fifty years ago, my great-grandfather decided to buy a llama. He must have learned that wool from llamas was more profitable than wool from sheep. The llama wool business turned out to be so successful, in fact, that my great-grandfather converted the family business to a full-fledged llama farm.

Before I began to live on the farm, I had held naive illusions of rural life. What could possibly be easier than feeding and grooming some animals? After I had settled into my new home, however, I realized that farm work was much more involved than I had expected. Collecting manure, for example, doesn't seem so bad when someone else does it on TV, but I had to get up before dawn every day to finish that chore before catching the bus to school.

School in the country was also not what I had expected. The school I attended had twenty students total: that's from first to twelfth grade, and I was the only student in my grade. We had one teacher who would occasionally lecture about a specific topic, but most of my learning came from studying textbooks on my own.

I don't mean to say that my life on the farm was a bad experience. I learned a lot about myself: for example, I'm not a morning person. I also learned about llamas' habits, such as spitting when they are unhappy. Most importantly, my mother and I got to spend a lot of time together during those days, for which I'm so grateful. Although I doubt I'll pursue a career in farming, I look forward to returning to the family farm for short visits.

全世界最美的课文

提分阅读海外升级版重磅来袭

意林重磅打造“高智商读本”，只为一心一意上名校的人！

《顶级名校课文大公开》《英国语文》《世界语文》，让你轻松成为世界名校学生。

《英国语文》

作者：《意林》编辑部

出版社：吉林摄影出版社

《英国语文》分为两卷，采用英汉双语对照形式，书的前半部分是中文，后半部分是英文。内容涵盖了《意林》编辑部从英国各中学课文中精选的两百多篇课文佳作，有成长励志故事，也有趣味科普文章，融故事性、知识性、趣味性于一体。有助于读者与国际课程接轨，领略英国风景，领悟精英文化。是初中、高中学生学习英语、学习作文、开拓视野以及备考留学的必备参考书。

《世界语文·德国卷》

（异域推理）（故事仙境）

作者：《意林》编辑部

出版社：吉林摄影出版社

《世界语文·德国卷》分两卷。文章均选自德国原版语文教材，由《意林》编辑部精心编排汇集而成。书中有金牌大师的绝妙演讲，有令人回味的趣味常识，还有大师手把手教你写小说。在这里你可以了解德国的各行各业，可是欣赏意味深远的隽永小诗，你可领悟德国的深邃文化，感受古典哲学的理性光芒，在阅读的同时深入思考，感悟人生。

《世界语文·美国语文》

作者：《意林》编辑部

出版社：吉林摄影出版社

《世界语文·美国语文》分两卷。文章均选自美国原版语文教材及高考真题中的经典阅读篇章，由《意林》编辑部精心编排汇集而成。在这里你可以了解美国别致的精彩故事，可以得到心灵的慰藉，你可以学会在美国生存的技能，感受独特的美国文化，在阅读的同时了解真实美国，学到实用技能。